Spiritual Treasure

44 True Stories of the Supernatural Grace of God

Roger Sapp

Spiritual Treasure
44 True Stories of the Supernatural Grace of God

Copies of this book are available from:

All Nations Ministries & Publications
PO Box 620, Springtown, Texas 76082
1-817-514-0653

Copies of this book may be ordered online from:
www.allnationsmin.org

www.christianhealingforum.com
(Post your prayer requests on this site and a number of people of faith will be praying for you.)

Spiritual Treasure
44 True Stories of the Supernatural Grace of God

Table of Contents

Spiritual Treasure
44 True Stories of the Supernatural Grace of God

Spiritual Treasure
44 True Stories of the Supernatural Grace of God

Acknowledgements

In particular, I would like to thank Jenny Beamer for her efforts in proof-reading this book. She is possibly the best editor that I have encountered in more than twenty years of publishing. Additionally, Tom and Jody Chauvin provided me some of their stories of healing. A few of those stories are in this first book and many more of their stories will be in the next collection of supernatural events of a gracious God. I would like to thank all the people on Facebook that encouraged me to write out these stories.

Spiritual Treasure
44 True Stories of the Supernatural Grace of God

Introduction

As I have done public ministry, I have shared a few of these testimonies to illustrate the functioning of the gifts of the Holy Spirit. Many years ago, I realized that people listening often remember the story but forget the teaching from which it came. Nevertheless, they learned something from the story.

A year or so ago, I wrote up a few of these stories to explain to younger Christians how the gifts of the Spirit may function. The reaction that I got was overwhelmingly positive. As a result, I decided to write out a few of the more memorable stories of the functioning of the Holy Spirit. This book is the result of that endeavor.

Since I have seen Jesus Christ compassionately heal tens of thousands of people, healing does dominate these stories. Only the most unusual of these stories are found in this book. Many healings - perhaps the great majority - in my ministry were similar enough to each other that I cannot separate them one from another any longer in my memory. These were important events in my life and the lives of those who received them. I welcome anyone who has a story that I should know about renewing my memory with their testimony of what occurred. Also, knowing that my memory and the actual facts may not be exactly the same, I invite anyone who is the subject of these stories to correct my possibly imperfect recollections.

I already have more stories in a list to write up to include in another book. There were many other stories that I could recount partially but I do not have sufficient details to tell them. If anyone reading this book has received something significant through a gift of the Holy Spirit - as a result of my service to Christ and the Church - and would not mind me recounting that story, please send it to me with as many details as you can remember. I have also encouraged those who have learned to minister Christ-centered healing as a result of my ministry to write up their stories of supernatural events in their service to Christ to include in another book.

The title of this book came as I considered who I was in relationship to these stories. The Lord seemed to point me to this particular verse.

He (Christ) said to them, "Therefore every scribe who has become a disciple of the kingdom of heaven is like a head of a household, who brings forth out of his treasure things new and old." (Matthew 13:52)

The Lord has been treasure to me. As a scribe who has become a disciple of the Kingdom, I entrust my treasure to you. I trust that you will treat it with respect and not be one of those that the Lord describes as "dogs" or "swine." The Lord says:

"Do not give what is holy to dogs, and do not throw your pearls before swine, lest they trample them under their feet, and turn and tear you to pieces." (Matthew 7:6)

I would like the readers of this book to keep in mind that these events occurred over many years of serving Christ. They were "mountain-top" experiences. There were some difficult "valleys" in between some of the "mountain-tops" that I do not describe in this book.

Just a handful of these events happened before I came to new conclusions on Christ as Healer. In other words, in my youthful service to Christ, I did see a few miraculous events but there was a great increase as I matured in my relationship with Him and understood better what He had taught His disciples about healing. The point is not to become distressed and impatient with God because you are not yet seeing everything that you would like to see. Put your trust in Christ. He has not forgotten you.

I would also like you to keep in mind that I believe that anyone can experience these kinds of supernatural events from the Lord. God is not a respecter of persons. This means that he does not show preference to one believer over another believer. I do not believe that I am significantly different than any other Christian. Christ does these things by His grace - His unmerited favor - and not a result of more effort, better character or anything else that has to do with me personally. It only has to do with His kindness, mercy and grace.

Blessings in Christ, Roger Sapp

Miracle in the Moonlight

In the first few months as a Christian, I experienced an amazing, miraculous event that was coupled with an inner knowing of what to do. I was a young soldier stationed in Wurzburg, Germany. I was saved by Jesus in a Christian coffeehouse that we attended regularly. In February, there was a Christian friend - who also attended this coffeehouse - who was leaving the Army and returning home. He needed a ride to the Frankfurt Rhein-Main Airport. I volunteered to drive him there.

It was not a long trip. It took about an hour and a half to get to the airport from where we lived. He didn't need to be there until after 8 pm, so we left at about 6 pm. My wife Ann and our two young children - one was a baby - came along with us. We arrived at the airport about 7:30 pm. We said our goodbyes and he went into the terminal.

We left the terminal and got back on the Autobahn in a few minutes. In about a half hour, we had a noisy blowout of the front right tire. With some difficulties slowing down and steering the car, I got the car off the Autobahn to the shoulder. I got out of the car to examine the tire. I knelt down beside it to examine it carefully. The tire was very flat with the rim near the ground. Normally, this would not have been a problem, but I realized that I had taken the spare tire in for repairs a few days before because it was flat also. (At that time, I was a low-ranking soldier and we had a worn-out car with worn-out tires.) Absentmindedly, I had forgotten to pick up the repaired spare tire before leaving on this trip.

I got back into the car and explained the situation to my wife Ann. Whether or not this was accurate, we had been told that if your car broke down on the Autobahn, you could get a huge fine by the German police. We discussed not being able to afford a fine. It was also very cold and dark outside with only the light of a full moon to see. I was keeping the car engine running to keep my family warm. I didn't know how long I could do this and still have enough gasoline to drive us home. With all these unknowns in our minds, Ann and I started praying for Divine help.

We had prayed for 15 minutes or so and I began to feel strongly that I should drive on the flat tire. I knew that this would completely ruin the tire and might seriously damage the rim. However, the more that I prayed, the stronger I felt that I should drive on the flat tire. I told Ann that I felt that I should drive on the tire. She - seeing no other solution - reluctantly agreed.

I started driving slowly on the shoulder. There was a grinding noise that made me think that the metal rim was touching the ground at times. There was also a repeating "flabunk" sound happening. "Flabunk, flabunk, flabunk..." I was praying for this old car to hold up under the new strain that I was putting on it.

Fairly soon, there was no noise at all. I got going somewhat faster but was puzzled why I wasn't hearing any noise. Without any effort, I got back on the Autobahn and eventually was traveling at speeds in excess of 60 miles an hour with no evidence that anything was wrong with the tire. I drove 45 minutes on that tire and pulled into a parking space in front of the apartment building where we lived on the German economy. I got out of the car and walked over to the right side to look at the tire. It was no longer flat. I could not accept this. Thinking that I was tired, I walked completely around the car checking each of the tires to see if one of them was flat. All the tires were fine. I was dumbfounded and awed as I returned to the right front tire. We were hearing about the Second Coming of Christ in the coffeehouse during that season. I remembered hearing this verse:

"The sun shall be turned into darkness, And the moon into blood, Before the great and glorious day of the Lord shall come. And it shall be, that everyone who calls on the name of the Lord shall be saved." (Acts 2:20-21)

I looked up at the full moon and it did seem to be light red. I felt sure that the Lord was returning that night. I didn't sleep that night and made very sure that we were saved. We both prayed the sinner's prayer again. When the next morning arrived without Christ returning, I was both relieved and disappointed at the same time.

I got ready to go to work. When I went out to my car, I discovered that the front right tire was flat again and sitting on its rim. I was late to work that day but it was a great day. I experienced an awe of God's nearness all day. By the way, the rim was not damaged and the tire was not destroyed by me driving on it. We had it repaired.

A Lesson about the Holy Spirit and Healing

One of the first healings that I experienced in my early walk with Christ happened in a small church - about 40 people - in Enterprise, Alabama. I had been a Christian for a little over three years. I was working in the personnel office of the helicopter school at Fort Rucker as an enlisted soldier. The pastor of this church did not have a paid assistant and needed to go to a conference with his denomination. He knew that I had some ministry experience through being involved in coffeehouse ministry for the previous 3 years. He had made me his assistant and he asked me to substitute for him on a particular Sunday.

He had been preaching about the Baptism in the Holy Spirit to his congregation for several months but no one had received yet. He had been telling the people of this church that they needed to be holy in order to receive the Holy Spirit. This idea caused them to disqualify themselves. No one seemed to think that they were holy enough to receive the Holy Spirit.

When I got up that particular Sunday, I reversed this. I told them that the Holy Spirit comes to work in us to make us holy. I told the congregation that the Father would give them the Holy Spirit even if they were not yet holy because He knew that the Holy Spirit would help them in those areas. I told them that they needed to receive the Holy Spirit if they still had trouble with sinning. This, of course, allowed everyone to qualify themselves to receive.

The pastor's wife was the first to receive. I laid hands on her and she began to pray fluently in a language that she didn't know. Secondly, the pastor's son received the Holy Spirit in a similar fashion. After these two key members of the congregation had received - obviously offering approval of what I had preached - the Holy Spirit fell on the entire church. Without anyone praying for them, the entire church was praying in languages that they did not know. This was the second time that I had seen the Holy Spirit do this. (I will write up the other account soon.) There was excitement all over. Thank you, Jesus.

I did not have healing happening predictably or reliably at this time. However, I had mentioned healing briefly in my message that Sunday morning. Seeing the whole church receive the Holy Spirit - without prayer - had certainly made me strongly aware of God's power and presence. In that atmosphere of faith and expectation, a woman came up to me and showed me her hands. Her joints were all swollen and her fingers were misshapen due to arthritis. She asked for prayer. I put my hands on her hands and prayed.

I didn't feel anything happen and I didn't know to ask her if she felt anything. I had little experience with healing and didn't know what to do if something didn't seem to be happening. That seemed to be the case to me. However, she didn't seem to react as if nothing had happened. She seemed to think that she was healed despite not seeing anything change. This was a good early lesson on healing for me because when I saw her at the Wednesday night service, she showed me her very normal hands. She had been healed. Thank you, Jesus.

When the pastor returned from the conference and discovered that the church had all received the Baptism in the Holy Spirit (including his wife and son) and that there had been a healing, he joked with me and said, "I'm going to have to go away more often."

The First Creative Miracle

A number of years ago, I was an avid runner (50 miles a week). On one of my runs home, I noticed a Christian bumper sticker on a neighbor's car. Since I didn't know these particular neighbors, I made a mental note to go introduce myself and my wife to them. I did this later in the day and immediately had strong fellowship with this young husband and wife. They were in their mid-thirties and my wife and I were somewhat younger, but we did have a lot in common with them and noted that in our first encounter with them. They invited us inside their house and offered us coffee to drink, which we accepted. We were seated across a coffee table from them. At some point in our fellowship, the man asked if we could pray with each other and we agreed.

He began to pray and within seconds of that time, I heard the Lord say to me, "Put your left hand on her ear." I reached across the coffee table with my left hand and put it on her ear. I immediately felt a surge of divine electricity pass from my hand into her ear. This was the first time that I had ever experienced something like this in healing. With excitement, I said, "The Lord has just healed your left ear." She looked up at me with a very puzzled expression. Her reaction caused me to doubt. I felt that maybe there was nothing wrong with her ear but I didn't express my doubt out loud for them to hear. She said, "You said that the Lord has healed my left ear, but you didn't have your hand on my left ear but on my right ear." She was right. I had reached across the table and had put my left hand on her right ear, not her left ear. She went on to say, "There is nothing wrong with my left ear, but I was born without hearing in my right ear and don't have any of the normal things that allow people to hear. I don't have an ear drum. I don't even have nerves in that ear." That made me feel better but there was no obvious change in the ear. However, the next morning she woke up with normal hearing in that ear. Everything that was missing was supplied by the Lord. The Lord had given her a creative miracle.

My early experience with the Lord in healing was laden with misunderstanding about healing. One of those misunderstandings was that in order for a healing or miracle to happen, a revelation like this was needed in advance. While I do occasionally get words of knowledge for healings and miracles like this, 99% of the tens of thousands of healings and miracles I have seen have not involved a word of knowledge. Anyone can receive a healing or a miracle by coming to Jesus as Healer in simple faith. However, things do happen like this because our God is very gracious.

Six Days of Divine Guidance

At the end of my second year as a Christian, I had an unusual series of events happened in a six-day period initiated by the Lord through His divine guidance. This guidance involved two dreams, words coming to me as I prayed, a knowledge of Scripture, unexpected circumstances, and precise timing of events.

Day One: I was a young soldier stationed in Wurzburg, West Germany, and living with my wife and young children on the German economy. It was my practice to rise at 4 am to pray and study the Scriptures for several hours before reporting to work. On a particular Monday morning as I was praying, I heard the Lord say one word to me. He said, "Dallas." I went to high school in the Dallas area and consider it my hometown. Despite this, I did not know what to think about the Lord saying this to me.

Several hours later, I got into my car to go to work. I turned on the radio which was tuned to the American Forces Network. The first word that I heard through the car speakers was "Dallas." It was in the middle of a sentence but it was the first word that I heard from the radio that morning. I knew that hearing "Dallas" again was no coincidence. At that point, I knew - with a strong inner conviction - that the Lord wanted me to go to Dallas. I felt that it was urgent.

After arriving at work, I called my wife to let her know that I believed that the Lord wanted me to go to Dallas. I had not told her about the first word that came in prayer. So I told her about hearing "Dallas" from the Lord in prayer and then hearing it in the car. Her first question was "Why does the Lord want you to go to Dallas?" I told her that I didn't know but felt that it was urgent. I was, at the time, a low-ranking soldier, which meant that we didn't have much money. We didn't have money for any of us to fly back to Dallas on a commercial flight. My only option was to fly "space available" on a military aircraft. Because of so many unknowns, Ann and I decided that I should do this alone.

During my lunch hour, I went to the company head-quarters office to formally request leave, which is permission to be away from the Army. I asked for all the leave time that I had available which was ten days. When the First Sergeant saw my leave form, he said to me, "You do know that you have to request leave two weeks in advance. You want to start your leave tomorrow. This is not going to happen." I said, "First Sergeant, I want to leave as soon as I can. If I can't leave for two weeks, then I guess that will have to be okay." I left the office and went back to work. An hour later, the First Sergeant phoned where I worked and said to me, "The Commander has signed your leave. You can go tomorrow." When I heard this, it seemed very much like another validation that I should go.

Day Two: Because I had very little money to use for traveling, a Christian friend drove me to Frankfurt Rhein-Main Airport. I arrived in the early afternoon. I spoke to the Space-Available (Space-A) Air Force clerk in the terminal. He gave me some bad news about how many people were waiting for a flight. The terminal was full of military personnel and their families waiting for a Space-A flight back to the USA. There were more than two hundred military people and their families waiting in the terminal. All of them were higher up on the Space-A list than I was. I asked the clerk how long would it take for me to be at the top of the list. He says "Two to three weeks." Since I only had ten days to make this trip, I knew that this would not work. I would use up all my leave waiting in the airport for a flight that may not happen at all.

Because I simply didn't know what to do, I prayed in the airport for help and guidance from the Lord. This time of prayer went on intermittently for six or seven hours. During that time, there were two military airplanes that had some extra seats. I watched two or three Space-A passengers get on each of these flights.

At about 9 pm, there was an announcement that there would be no more flights going out for that day. Just about everyone left the terminal. I suspected that most of them, if not all, checked into the military hotel for the night. I seriously considered doing this also. However, as I considered this, I lost my peace, which is a way for the Lord to tell me not to do anything. I decided to stay in the airport terminal. Moments after I made this decision, my peace returned, confirming to me that I should stay in the terminal.

Without any explanation from the Space-A clerks, at about 10 pm, there was another Space-A call for a flight going back to the USA. There were only 3 spaces available on this flight, but just about everyone ahead of me on the list had left the terminal. I was the last person that got on this flight back to the USA. This was another amazing verification to me that I was supposed to go to Dallas.

Day Three: I arrived in the USA and obtained on that same day a Space-A flight to Carlswell Air Force Base in Fort Worth, Texas. (Presently, this is a reserve Naval Air Station.) This was about 30 miles from where my wife's parents lived. I arrived unexpectedly at their home late on that day. My wife's parents asked me why I was in Dallas. I told them that I felt that the Lord wanted me to come. I also told them of several practical matters that I wanted to accomplish while I was there. They offered me a place to stay in their home while I was in Dallas.

I was very tired from traveling. I went to bed in their guest bedroom. During the night, I had an unusual dream. In the dream, I was in the same bedroom. I was lying on the same bed and wrestling with an invisible figure that was stronger than I was. In the dream, I began to command this invisible figure to release me in the name of Jesus. Eventually, it weakened and released me. I woke up from this dream and wonder what it was about. Shortly after the dream, I went back to sleep.

Day Four: The next morning, I woke up with awareness that the dream was highly significant but without knowing what to do about it. I prayed about it and also for God to show me why I was in Dallas. Despite having the amazing circumstance of getting on the Space-A flight in Frankfurt, Germany, I still didn't know why I was in Dallas.

Later in the day, I began to take care of the things that I knew I should accomplish while in Dallas but knew that was not the reason why God has sent me. Nothing else happened in an unusual way until I went to bed. I had another dream. It was nearly the same dream as the previous night. I was wrestling against an invisible figure that was stronger than I was. However, this time this invisible figure was trying to keep me from seeing something that was written on my right shoulder. It was preventing me from turning my head to the right so I could get a good look at what was written on my shoulder. Again, I used the name of Jesus and commanded it to release me. It seemed to weaken and I turned my head to the right and saw clearly what was written on my shoulder. It was the word "Transie." I immediately woke up from the dream but had no idea what "Transie" meant. I speculated for an hour or so what this might mean, but eventually came to the conclusion that I really didn't know what possible significance this word might have. Eventually, I went back to sleep.

Day Five: I woke up again with a strong awareness that these two dreams were highly significant but I still had no understanding of what they meant. I still had no idea what "Transie" meant. I prayed quite a bit that day for understanding of the dreams and for clarity about why I was in Dallas. I did recognize on that day something that I had learned from study of the Scriptures. I had learned from the story of Joseph in Genesis - who interpreted Pharaoh's dreams - that two dreams coming close together means that they would happen soon.

Later that afternoon, my wife's parents got a call from my father. My father and mother were in Dallas on a business trip and my father wanted to say hello to my wife's parents. They told my father that I was also in Dallas. I got on the phone with my father and I suggested that we have a meal together. However, my father did not want to do this. He told me that they were leaving early in the morning and there wasn't time to do this. I asked him if he intended to have breakfast before leaving in the morning. It was clear that he didn't really want to see me.

Nevertheless, I insisted on having breakfast with them because I thought that this might be the reason why I was in Dallas. While I grew up in Dallas, my parents had moved to Lafayette, Louisiana, after I had left home. For us both to be in Dallas at the same time seemed to be an unusual event. My father finally agreed for me to have breakfast with them before they flew home. I went to bed that night praying that I would not miss God's purpose for me being in Dallas.

Day Six: I got up early to meet my father and mother in a restaurant near Love Field Airport. At this time, this airport was not a public airport as it is today. It was used primarily by business people with their own airplanes. I met my father and mother for breakfast. My father was very cold towards me and it was reasonably clear that he didn't want to see me.

My father and I had not gotten along well during my teenage years. I was not a bad kid. I had decent grades in high school. I never got into any trouble. I was an Eagle Scout and a camp counselor. Nevertheless, I was unable to please my father during those years. He could not tolerate me having different opinions about anything. He was unable to leave these matters alone. He would often bring them up to start a fight with me. He was also highly critical of anything and everything that I was doing.

I don't remember my father ever saying anything positive to me during those years. This made me highly reactive to him. I was ready to argue with him at a moment's notice. My mother had done what she could to be a peacemaker between us. She would even serve us dinner at different times. She knew that anytime my father had an opportunity, he would pick a fight with me. She knew also that I would never back down from an argument with my father.

When I had received Christ as Savior, the people who had led me to Christ taught me the importance of forgiveness. They had also taught me the right and wrong way to ask for forgiveness. They had taught me that if I wanted real forgiveness from someone, that I should never bring up what they had done wrong towards me. I should keep the entire focus on what I had done wrong. I had written letters asking for forgiveness to my mother and father during the first year after I had received Christ as Savior.

I had also seen in the Scripture that God wanted me to honor my father and mother. My mother was no problem but honoring my father was an act of faith. My desire to have breakfast with my parents was partially motivated by a desire to honor them and partially because I was feeling that this might be the reason why the Lord sent me to Dallas.

So as we were having breakfast together, my father once again tried to pick a fight with me. He said without any provocation, "You Charismatics are tearing up churches all over." He said "Charismatics" as if it was a dirty word. He was clearly trying to insult me. My father and mother were Baptists at this time and had rejected my experience of receiving the Holy Spirit. They were particularly hostile towards the supernatural prayer language - speaking in tongues - that I had received and used daily.

I replied to my father, "Dad, who is actually tearing up the churches? Is it those who are yielding to the Holy Spirit or those who are resisting the Holy Spirit?"

My father's expression immediately changed to anger, his face reddened and the veins in his neck became very visible. In a display of disgust towards me, he grabbed the newspaper on the table and opened it between him and me. My mother leaned over towards me so my father could not see her behind the newspaper. She whispered, "Don't say anything else." I felt sorry that this had happened. It was not what I wanted. I was sitting there wondering if I had done the wrong thing.

Suddenly, my father turned the newspaper around so I could see what he had been reading. He had providentially opened it to the "Religion" section. In a large headline, the paper said something like "Charismatic Baptist Church Thrown Out of Baptist Convention." The story outlined that a large Charismatic Baptist Church in Dallas was using every means at their disposal to remain in the Baptist organization, but the organization was forcing them out for no other reason than the fact that they believed that the gifts of the Holy Spirit were functioning today.

I said to my father after seeing this newspaper story, "Dad, who is creating this disunity? It is not this

Charismatic Baptist church. They are trying to maintain the unity without compromising what they believe to be true. It is the non-Charismatics that are breaking the union."

My father did not say anything else about this church but seemed to get my point. He certainly had calmed down. Then he shocked me by saying, "I spoke in tongues not too long ago." What an amazing moment that was. He explained to me that he and my mother had argued over something and this had really depressed him. He had to make a short trip in his car for business. While he was in the car, he began to pray about the argument with my mother. He felt some strong emotion and then heard himself praying in a language unknown to him. It had scared him so he immediately quit doing it. The atmosphere at that table was charged with peace and the presence of God. For an amazing fifteen minutes, I became a teacher to my very humble father. I taught him about using the supernatural language that he had received from the Lord. He seemed to soak up every word.

Then just as suddenly as he had admitted that he had spoken in tongues, I felt him stiffen and not be receptive any longer. He said, "Roger, we need to get to the airport. It is time for us to leave." I said, "Dad, I want to see you off. I will follow you over there." He then said to me that this was not necessary. We could say goodbye in the restaurant. I said, "No, Dad, I want to see you off at the airport." It was in my heart to spend as long with them as possible. I wanted to do my best to honor them. My father reluctantly agreed to me following them to the airport.

In a few minutes, I parked my car near the terminal at Love Field Airport. My father turned in the rental car that he was using. My parents prepared to board the private airplane. While they were very uncomfortable with hugging at that time, I hugged them anyway. They got on the airplane and in a few minutes they were on their way back to Lafayette, Louisiana.

While I was sure that the Lord had brought me to Dallas for this amazing 15 minutes with my father, I was not sure that I had done everything that the Lord had wanted. The circumstances were so unusual that I felt it must be for that reason but I was unclear if I had done what the Lord wished me to do. The situation felt unfinished as if there was still something else that needed to happen but my parents were gone now.

I slowly walked back to the car seriously considering if I had missed the will of God in this situation. I glanced up toward where the car was parked. To my amazement, I saw the word "Transie" in large letters. On the side of the terminal, it should have said, "Dallas Transient Airport" but the last two letters, the "n" and "t," had fallen off the word "Transient." You could still see the outline of where these letters were originally but they were missing. So the sign actually said, "Dallas Transie Airport."

In that moment, I felt the strong presence of the Lord and was filled with joy and the knowledge that I had done exactly what God had wanted. I knew that I was in the perfect will of God. I also realized that if I had chosen not to honor my father and mother by having breakfast with them and following them afterward to the airport, I would have never seen the word "Transie." I returned to

Germany in the next few days with joy and told this story in the fellowship of believers that I attended.

There were long-term positive changes in my relationship with my father. In the next three decades, we never again had an argument. Sometimes, we had long discussions about spiritual things. While there were still differences of opinion, we were reconciled permanently through this event. It was an event that had been inspired entirely by the Lord. Thank you, Lord Jesus.

A Young Boy's Blind Eye Opened

This is one of the first few miracles that I experienced in my early walk with the Lord. In a Sunday night service, we prayed for a 9-year-old boy who had been born without sight in his right eye. He was born with that eye damaged beyond repair. It had scar tissue over the back of the eye and no light could pass through it. The retina was also detached and there were other problems as well.

On the previous Sunday night, there had been a healing of a woman who had one leg much shorter than the other due to having polio as a child. During prayer, her leg shot out at least four inches and she was able to walk normally. This had inspired the parents of the 9-year-old boy to bring him for prayer this night.

The atmosphere was literally electric. You could put your hands in the air and feel the power of God like electricity in the air. We laid hands on the boy and within seconds of that time, it seemed as if a bolt of lightning went through those who were praying and the entire congregation. There was a nearly simultaneous and surprised "Oh!" through the congregation as we felt this happen.

They gave the boy a New Testament and covered his good eye. He read briefly from the New Testament as joy and praise to God came from the congregation. His sight was restored in that eye.

In the next week the boy's parents took him to an ophthalmologist who checked the formerly blind eye. It now had perfect vision despite the fact that nothing had changed physically in the eye. It was impossible for the boy to see through the eye naturally and yet he was able to see perfectly.

This miracle helped me to understand that God is not limited to simply fixing what is broken in healing. God can bypass the problem all together and simply give to us what is needed.

Soldier Protected by a Word of Knowledge

As a US Army Chaplain, I was often involved with soldiers who had gotten themselves in trouble with the chain of command. In most cases, it was simply a matter of them doing something that was insubordinate-- committing a petty crime such as theft, or doing something unwise that gained them the negative attention of their commanding officer. However, in a small percentage of cases that I saw, it was the chain of command that was wrong and not the soldier. Among other roles, a Chaplain is an advocate for the soldier to the chain of command. This means that a good Chaplain might have to challenge officers who outrank him in order to insure that an innocent soldier is not unfairly treated.

A young woman soldier - a private in rank - came to me who was in trouble with her Company Commander and Battalion Commander. The Battalion Commander - a woman also - had decided to Court Martial her for telling a "lie" about the Company Commander making sexual advances to her. The Company Commander strongly denied the young woman soldier's charge. The Battalion Commander was backing him without even hearing the young woman's story. It was not too hard to see why. The Battalion Commander and the Company Commander were of the same minority ethnic group. They were friends. The Battalion Commander was known to be "grooming" this particular Company Commander for higher rank and responsibilities. He was openly a favorite of the Battalion Commander.

Despite knowing this, I was very neutral in this situation because I didn't know who was telling the truth. However, after questioning the young woman soldier, I realized that she knew way too much about the Company Commander. She had many details of his personal life. She had obviously been in his quarters because she was able to describe - in detail - personal items of the Company Commander. He should have never allowed her to come into his quarters. It was highly improper and against regulations. She even knew about what brand of liquor he liked to drink. It was obvious that she had detailed knowledge about him that could only come by him telling her and being in his quarters. Relationships between enlisted personnel and officers are always forbidden, especially if the enlisted soldier is under the command of the officer. She was under his command. It is the responsibility of the officer to avoid putting himself in a situation like this. It is certainly a way to destroy your career as an officer.

I believed what this young woman soldier was telling me. I went to the Battalion Commander to inform her of the details that I had gathered in support of this young woman soldier's story. I was met with strong resistance from her. She did not want me to tell her or anyone else about this. She wanted to silence and punish this low-ranking woman soldier and didn't even want to know her side of the story.

She asked me not to say anything to anyone about this and to meet with her in two hours and she would show me that the young woman soldier was lying. If the Battalion Commander had real evidence that the young woman soldier was lying, I did want to hear it. However, I believed that it would be hard to convince me because of all the detailed information that this woman soldier had about her Company Commander and his quarters.

Two hours later, I reported back to the Battalion Commander's office. The Battalion Commander, the Company Commander and a young male soldier were there when I arrived. The Battalion Commander said to me, "I want you to hear what this soldier has to say." The young male soldier told me that he had heard the young woman soldier say that she was going to "get" the Company Commander by accusing him of "hitting" on her. Just after he said this, the Holy Spirit gave me a word of knowledge. The Holy Spirit said, "Three hundred fifty dollars."

I knew immediately that the Battalion Commander and the Company Commander had paid this soldier to lie. I said to the Battalion Commander, "I would like to talk with this soldier alone for a few minutes." We went outside the office and I said to the soldier, "Three hundred fifty dollars." The color drained from his face. I left him outside the office and returned to my own office to pray for a good outcome in this situation.

The Battalion Commander called me on the phone and asked me to return to her office. I arrived and she asked me to sit down. She knew that I knew that they had paid him to lie. She said to me, "What can we do to satisfy you in this situation?" I said to her, "I want you to drop the charges against this young soldier and immediately move her to another battalion. I want this to happen today." She said, "Done." I went on to say, "I know that the Company Commander has crossed some serious lines here. I am not asking you to charge him with anything but I think that you ought to make him very aware that you will not tolerate such behavior again." She said to me, "We have already had that talk, Chaplain. I assure you that I will not tolerate the slightest error in judgment from him again." I stood and said, "Thank you, Ma'am" and saluted. She returned my salute and said, "Dismissed" and I left her office. She did drop the charges and moved the young woman soldier to another battalion that day. I served with her as my Battalion Commander for another year. She implemented every one of my suggestions to her during that time. She never asked me how I knew about the "Three hundred fifty dollars." Perhaps she didn't want to know.

A Merciful Creative Miracle

As I began to have a new understanding about healing drawn from Christ as my example, I had a particular event happen in my office that revealed to me a number of things about the power of God expressed through His mercy. At the time, I was preparing to retire from the US Army Chaplaincy and was serving my last months on active duty as the Army Hospital Chaplain. I had not yet seen a lot of healing but that was starting to change dramatically.

I had a Christian couple coming for marital counseling. The man was on active duty and held the rank of Sergeant. He was also a licensed minister with a large denomination and serving as a part-time, unpaid associate minister in a church local to us. This kind of thing is not uncommon in the US Army. (I had done this for years before I had become a Chaplain.)

This Sergeant was in trouble with his church and with his wife. He had been exposed in at least three different affairs with women in the church. Because he had used his position in the church in this negative way, the church leadership felt that it was necessary to remove him from leadership and from the church. They disciplined him publicly and kicked him out of the church.

The first time I met him, he was very humble and contrite about what he had done. His wife was a godly woman but was she was very hurt and angry over this--with him and with the church. The church had kicked her out also and she was not guilty of doing anything wrong.

When they first came to see me, the man would say things that sounded like he was justifying what he had done. He would say, "I just wanted to have a child." Well, this would infuriate her because he had married her knowing that she was unable to have children. She had had a complete hysterectomy eight years previously and did not have any reproductive organs. This statement of his made no real sense to me and I knew it was stirring up trouble between them. I would say to him, "If I were you, I would not say that any longer. There is no excuse for what you have done."

Their interactions in that first counseling session became increasingly loud and angry. He would demand forgiveness from her and she resented it a great deal. She was highly reactive to him. I decided after the first counseling session that I would need to meet with them separately.

I had a number of sessions with him where I helped him deal with a false image of what a real man is like. He had, through exposure to an unfaithful father, a deep misunderstanding of what a real man was like. He thought that real men would have to be unfaithful to their wives in order to satisfy their strong sexual needs. I helped him realize that this was a lie from the devil and got him to deeply repent over this.

The wife met with me also during the same period of time. Her primary issue was forgiveness of her husband, the women that he had been sexually involved with, and the church that she felt had mistreated her. I gave her an assignment to bring to the first counseling session without her husband. I asked her to write down everyone who had hurt her.

She arrived at the first counseling appointment with her list. It had about fifteen names on it, if I remember correctly. I spoke with her about her need to obey the Lord concerning forgiving others. I made it plain to her that forgiving them was for her sake and not because they deserved it. I wrote a simple prayer at the top of her list "I forgive_____ for the pain that they have caused me in the name of Jesus." I got her to start at the top of the list and verbally forgive each of the people who had harmed her. As she did this, I agreed with her in prayer.

This was obviously meaningful to her because she wept as she forgave each person. She slowly worked her way through the list. When she had reached about halfway in the list, I started feeling electricity - the power of God - in my hands. I had only felt this manifestation twice before. I was unsure about what to do so I quietly asked the Lord what to do. I felt after that prayer that I should be patient and let her work her way completely through the list before doing anything else. As I waited and continued to agree with her forgiveness prayers, the sensation of power continually increased and felt like it was flowing across my back, down my arms and into my hands. It was living electricity.

She got through with her list. I asked her if it would be alright for me to put my hands on her head and pray for her. I was aware that this was something that ministers in her denomination would probably not do. She gave me permission. I put my very electric hands on her head and quietly prayed for her. I felt the power of God move from my hands and into her head.

After about 5 minutes or so, my hands felt completely normal again. I sat down in my chair and we began to talk. However, within a few seconds, her eyes rolled back so all I saw was the white of her eyes. Her eyelids began to quiver strongly. She fell off the couch where she was sitting. She started making loud sounds like "Oooooh" and "Aaaaah" from the floor of my office as she writhed around on the floor. I was totally unprepared for this.

My office was in the hospital and the doors were open to the hallway. I felt sure that everyone in the offices up and down the hallway could hear this and someone would come to investigate. So I called my Chaplain's Assistant into the room. I said, "Sergeant, you'd better come in here right now." He was also a minister of the Gospel and when he came in, we briefly discussed what was happening with this woman.

We closed the office doors to the outside because she was still making a lot of noise. We laid hands on her and many evil spirits were leaving her. After 15 minutes or so, she seemed to come out of this and got back up on the couch. However, this was short-lived because she again fell off the couch and was on the floor writhing around and making the same noises. The Sergeant and I continued to minister deliverance from evil spirits to her. She seemed to come out of this after a while and got back up on the couch.

Shortly after the second time, we went through this a third time but this time it was different. She fell off the couch but was not making the noises. Instead of writhing around, she seemed very peaceful, much like she was asleep. The Sergeant and I saw a line of bright light appear across her head from ear to ear and then move slowly down her body all the way to her feet and then back up her body to her forehead. We discussed where we were seeing the light. This happened three times with each time taking about two minutes. On the third time, when the light reached her forehead, it disappeared.

Shortly after the line of light disappeared, she sat up on the floor and said, "I feel great!" She did look different. She had brightness on her face that was not there before. I had a sense that she had been healed of something, but I didn't really know what. I was sure that she had been delivered from demons. She left my office victorious that day but that was not the end of the story.

She came back a few weeks later to share with me that she had been healed of "Grave's Disease." She had not told me that she had this illness, but I rejoiced with her over her healing. Another week or two passed and she came to see me again and told me with excitement that she had had a menstrual period. When she said this, it went over my head and I didn't understand at first. When she saw that I didn't get the significance of this, she said it very plainly to me. "I had a complete hysterectomy 8 years ago, but God has given me my reproductive organs back." I took this in with amazement. Later, in private, I sincerely thanked the Lord for this creative miracle.

Within a few months of this time, she was pregnant. This couple had a bouncing baby boy nine months later. Keep in mind what had happened here. God heard the cry of a sinful but believing man's heart about his desire to have a child, and the desire of a godly woman to do the right thing despite being hurt. God granted them a miracle baby boy, despite the fact that they were not getting along at the time and each of them still had serious issues to resolve. How great is mercy and kindness of our God!

Voodoo Woman Delivered and Saved

Just before I retired from the US Army, I was serving as the Installation Hospital Chaplain. It was a nice gig in that my wife Ann worked in the same hospital - as a civilian registered nurse - about a hundred feet away from my office. On a particular day, my wife Ann started sharing the Good News with a young woman who was working in her area. As she shared the Good News about Jesus Christ, this young woman had never really heard or understood what Jesus had done for her at the cross. She was amazed and wanted to become a Christian.

She had grown up on a Caribbean island and her family's religion was Voodoo. She had not even been exposed to the synthesis of Christian ideas and Voodoo that is common in the Caribbean. She only knew Voodoo. Ann intuitively knew that she should not try to pray with this young woman in the open area of her workplace. She decided to send her down the hall to my office. She called me about this, told me about this woman's background, and let me know that this young woman was coming.

She arrived at my office and introduced herself and said she wanted to become a Christian. Of course, I was delighted to pray with her. I intended to lead her in a typical sinner's pray confessing her belief in what Christ had done for her at the cross. However, she could not pray at all. She could not say anything. She started having some demonic manifestations. (I locked my door and called Ann for prayer support.)

I recognized these manifestations as demonic and commanded in the name of Jesus for these evil spirits to cease their activity and to leave her. She started getting a massive deliverance from evil spirits. She choked out, coughed out, yawned out, sighed out, sneezed out, retched out, and occasionally screamed out evil spirits. (When evil spirits are cast out, they leave most often through the mouth.) This went on for at least three hours.

At different intervals during the three hours, I stopped and asked her to try praying again. She couldn't pray. I asked her to just try calling on Jesus for help. She could not say "Jesus" at all for at least two hours. However, during the third hour, she started having freedom to pray. At the end of the three hours, she was able to say the name of Jesus. When she was able to do this, much more deliverance from evil spirits followed quickly. I made sure that she had prayed the sinner's prayer and had received Christ as Savior before we were done that day.

Ann and I met with her - away from the hospital - and ministered more deliverance to her and helped her receive the Baptism in the Holy Spirit. The last we heard she was joyfully serving Christ. Thank you, Lord.

A Word of Knowledge Through A Dream

I had a friend who called me about a woman that he was counseling. He had reached an impasse with her and there had been no improvement in her emotional outlook for some time. He wanted to refer her to me for at least one session so I could give him feedback on my perceptions about her and her emotional outlook. She had agreed to this.

She arrived at my house where I had my office. The moment that I saw her, I realized that I had seen her in a dream the week before. In the dream, she was angry, depressed and strongly reactive to her husband and teenage sons. She complained bitterly about them. She really didn't like them. After hearing her complaints about them, I said to her, "Why don't you tell me your real problem?" She said (in the dream), "My father molested me."

I decided to let this situation play out like the dream. I asked her to tell me what was bothering her. Just like the dream, she complained bitterly about her husband and teenage sons. She was angry, depressed and did say that she thought that she constantly overreacted to the male members of her family. When she had done this, I asked "Anything else?" and she said that she couldn't think of anything else. At that moment, I decided to tell her that I had had a dream about her the previous week. I told her how the dream was very like what I was experiencing with her on that day. I then told her about the question that I asked her in the dream "Why don't you tell me your real problem?" and then I told her how she had answered in the dream, "My father molested me."

When she heard this, she started sobbing. I laid my hands on her head gently and felt a lot of power flow to her for a few minutes. A few minutes later, she seemed much more at peace. Shortly after this, she left my office. A few weeks later, I heard from my friend that her depression had disappeared completely. She was no longer angry and reactive to the male members of her family. She was a very different woman. Christ healed this brokenhearted woman.

The Healing of a Satanist

Before having the breakthrough in understanding about Christ as the perfect model of healing ministry (that has led to tens of thousands of healings), I had one or two healings each year for a period of about twenty years. One of those healings occurred as I served as the US Army Chaplain to the 716th Military Police Battalion. At the time, this unit was stationed at Fort Riley, Kansas.

One of my responsibilities as the Military Police Chaplain was to minister to the Installation Detention Facility. This was simply a jail for soldiers who had been accused and/or convicted of crimes. There were prisoners who had earned the right - through good behavior - to be housed with other prisoners in a larger area that had bunk beds. Good behavior gave these prisoners more privileges, such as: being able to spend more time exercising, watching television, access to the jail's library, and being able to come to the prison chapel for services on Sundays.

On the other hand, a few prisoners - who were violent or demonstrated other bad behavior - were locked up by themselves for their own safety and the safety of the other prisoners. At any given time, this jail would have up to five or six potentially violent prisoners locked up in individual cells.

It was my practice to visit this jail minimally three times a week and lead a Christian worship service on Sunday mornings there. On my visits, I would make sure to have face-to-face contact with each prisoner. This would include those prisoners locked up in individual cells. Most of these men in individual cells would speak with me each time I visited. However, there was one prisoner who would never speak to me. He was a large, muscular man. According to the documents from his trial, he believed himself to be a worshiper of Satan. He had been violent and had threatened murder during his trial. He had been tried and convicted for refusing to obey an order and possession of an illegal drug. He had to be restrained during the trial. He was waiting to be transferred to Fort Leavenworth, Kansas, which has a large military prison.

After a few times of trying to get him to speak to me unsuccessfully, I asked the Lord to do something to change this situation. The next time I came by his cell, he was lying on his bunk, writhing around, holding his head, groaning and crying. I asked him what was wrong and for the first time, he spoke to me. He said, "I have migraine headaches." I asked him "Have the guards given you anything for it?" He said, "Yes, but it hasn't helped." I said, "Can I pray for you?" He said loudly, "Anything. Anything." and writhed in pain upon his bunk. I said out loud, "Lord Jesus, I ask that you help this man."

A few seconds later, he looked up and said, "The pain is gone." He sat up and had an amazed look on his face. He said it again but much slower, "The pain is completely gone." I said to him, "Yes, Jesus loves you and has died for you to be whole." He shook his head as if he couldn't believe it. I decided to leave him alone with his thoughts. I prayed for him each day. During the next week, he requested a Bible. I gave him a Bible and a book that outlined how to study the Bible. The week following that week, I asked him if he wanted to receive Christ as

Savior. He said that he did and I prayed with him to invite Christ into His life. He was born again.

Eventually, he was transferred to Fort Leavenworth. I occasionally got letters from him and he was growing as a Christian. He attended Chapel at Leavenworth regularly and apparently was telling the story of his healing from a migraine headache. Beyond that, he wasn't having migraine headaches any longer. Thank you, Lord.

Healing of Sinus Infections

From the time that I was 9 years old, I suffered from sinus infections. I suspect that I averaged 5 or 6 infections each year. Sometimes, a sinus infection would go on for months despite taking medication for it. I often had a horrible burning or throbbing sensation behind my eyes and in the back of my head. As a young enlisted soldier, then later as an artillery officer, and then as an Army chaplain, I simply couldn't stop working because I was in pain and didn't feel well. Despite believing theoretically in healing, I often endured through a sinus infection by alternating different over-the-counter pain medications. I also was in the habit of going to the gym and working out to heat up my body. This caused my sinuses to clear and stopped the pain temporarily. During those days, I found that distance running would do the same thing so I averaged 40 miles a week running. I also spent time in steam rooms and saunas because they seemed to open my sinuses and relieved the pain I was experiencing. I endured sinus infections and the pain they produced for about 30 years.

As I neared retirement from the US Army Chaplaincy, I spent time seeking the Lord's guidance about what He wanted me to do in my future service to Him. During one of these occasions of prayer, the Lord asked me a question. He asked, "Why don't you receive Me as Healer in the same way that you received Me as Savior?" This question caught me by surprise for several reasons. First of all, I was not sick at that moment. Secondly, the question did not seem to be answering my inquiry about my future. Thirdly, the question implied that there was something wrong in the way that I was approaching healing. I didn't know how to respond. I think that I eventually said something like, "Lord, I don't understand the question so I don't know how to answer."

I knew that the Lord occasionally asks me questions because He wants me to think about what He is asking. I began to consider His question over the next few weeks. Christ, through the question, had invited me to compare what I believed about Christ being my Savior with what I believed about Christ being my Healer. He invited me to receive Him as Healer in the same way that I had received Him as Savior.

At that time (as I do now), I believed that Christ had died for my sins. I also believed that Christ had died for my sicknesses. Christ had done the work to be my Savior before I received Him as Savior. I realized that Christ had also done the work to be my Healer in the same way. The way that I received Christ as Savior happened in a very common pattern. I heard the Good News about what Christ had done for me at the cross. I believed it to be true. I prayed to receive Christ as my Savior. I was born again. My sins were wiped away. I was a new creation in Christ. In other words, I had believed and received Christ as my Savior. Then immediately afterward, I experienced the evidences of salvation for the first time. It was faith in Christ first, then came the initial experience of salvation.

I realized that I was not approaching healing in the same way. I had been waiting to be healed so that I could believe that Christ was my Healer. I had it backward. I needed to believe that Christ was already my Healer before I was healed. I needed to believe and receive Christ as my Healer, then I would experience healing. As

I came to understand this, I prayed and received Christ as my Healer.

I wish that I could write that everything was automatic after that prayer. However, that is not what I experienced. Within a few weeks of receiving Christ as my Healer, I developed a terrible sinus infection just before leaving. I felt horrible. I was running a fever and had a great deal of pain in my head. It was a little confusing but I realized that I need to make application of another truth. I reminded myself that Christ had invited me to compare my salvation with my healing. I knew that despite being saved, I didn't always feel saved. It was a matter of faith in Christ. I would focus on what Christ had done for me and the feelings of salvation would return. As a result of understanding this comparison, I made confessions that Christ was my Healer. I had a book of promises and I repeatedly confessed the promises concerning healing. When I would do this, I would be somewhat better for a short time but the symptoms would return strongly.

This was especially bad at night. I would be up battling the symptoms using Scripture and praise and worship during the night. Nevertheless, I did my best to continue to believe the Lord was my Healer. This battle continued for ten days. I was really no better after ten days than I was when I started. I was still experiencing fever and terrible headaches.

After ten days of battling this sinus infection, I realized that I was not making progress. I decided to reevaluate what I believed about healing. I asked myself if I believed that God has spoken to me. I had to answer, "Yes." I asked myself if the theology of healing that I had come to believe was correct. After some reflection, I affirmed that I believed that the Bible was teaching what I had come to believe. Shortly after this reevaluation, I confessed my faith in Christ as my Healer. This time, my confession was different. It was an absolute commitment to this truth without reservation. I said "Lord, I don't care how long healing takes or how healing comes, You are My Healer!" A second later, I was completely healed. All my symptoms disappeared immediately. I was completely well. (I have never had another sinus infection in more than two decades.)

Why did this work? I believe I was not receiving healing because I was still in the habit of wanting to be healed before I believed that Christ was my Healer. Without realizing it, I wanted proof that what I had come to believe was correct. I wanted healing to prove it to me that Christ was my Healer. When I made a strong commitment to the truth that Christ was already my Healer, then the manifestation of healing came. I believe that there are many people waiting to be healed so that they can believe that Christ is their Healer. (Believing in healing is not the same thing as believing that Christ is already your Healer.) They have it backwards and backwards does not work. We need to believe that Christ is already our Healer. We need to believe that, at the cross, He purchased healing for us. He is already our Healer, even if we have not yet believed and received what He has done.

Looking back, I can now see that I did get an answer to my inquiry about my future. The question I received pointed me to Christ as Healer. It straightened out my theology and focused me on the simplicity of Christ as

Healer. I have been doing healing ministry ever since those days. Thank you Lord for both healing me and teaching me about Yourself.

My Wife Ann Healed of Migraines and Asthma

Shortly after I had received healing of chronic sinus infections, my wife Ann responded in simple faith to the fact that I had been healed. She said to me, "If the Lord is willing to heal you, He is willing to heal me." This is, of course, an expression of a New Covenant truth. In the King James Version, it is expressed as "God is not a respecter of persons." It simply means that God shows no partiality, no favoritism. If one of us can receive healing, then all of us can.

Ann had struggled for decades with horrible migraine headaches. They came about once a month. She would be in serious pain and would lie down in a quiet, dark, and cool room. Any noise or light would create more pain for her. Often, Ann had to care for our children while she was dealing with one of these blinding headaches because I was a soldier and unavailable to help. I never heard Ann complain about her life. I never heard her complain about how much pain she was in.

These headaches would last 4 to 5 days but it would take her several days to recover from them. For about a week each month, I would lose my wife to pain. Despite the fact that I believed in healing and deliverance from evil spirits, I didn't seem able to help my poor, suffering wife. My prayers for her seemed ineffective. I often felt useless and powerless when she would be struggling in pain.

Ann also had serious issues with asthma. She struggled to breathe and had to use rescue inhalers and occasionally used stronger medications to help her breathe.

Because of a new understanding about healing, we prayed differently for Ann for the first time. We believed that the work of healing was already done for her through the sufferings of Christ. She accepted, for the first time, that Christ was already her Healer. We didn't try to get God to heal her. Instead, we believed that healing already belonged to her. We believed that Christ had taken upon Himself her headache pain. We believed that Christ had died for her asthma.

The result of this was absolutely amazing to us. When the time came -when she normally had a headache - there was no headache. She never again had one of these headaches. She has been free of these monthly migraine headaches for more than 17 years. Thank you, Jesus.

On the other hand, the asthma did not go away in the same fashion. She was somewhat better after that first time of prayer and went for a short season without her medications. However, the symptoms returned. We prayed again for her healing and once again, there was improvement and no need for medication for a season but the inability to breathe returned. However, over a short period of repeating prayer for her, she was showing good overall improvement. I would call her experience "Three steps forward, two back."

Within a six-month period, she was so much improved, that she no longer needed to use medication at all. By the time a year had passed, she no longer had any evidence of asthma. She has been free from asthma nearly as long as she has been free from migraine headaches.

Word of Wisdom About a Young Girl's Future

I believe that the word of wisdom is often confused with the word of knowledge. Both contain a supernatural revelation about a person or a situation. However, the word of knowledge is about the present but the word of wisdom is about the future. Both can flow together with a prophetic utterance or be ministered separately as simple words in a given situation.

I was preaching Christ as Healer and ministering healing in southern Louisiana in a church. We had seen the Lord heal quite a few people when a pre-teen girl presented herself. If I remember correctly, she was 11 years old. I asked her if she needed healing and she said that she just wanted me to pray for her. So I laid my hands on her and immediately got a word of wisdom. I saw her as a mature woman of God who had married in the will of God to a very successful and godly man who was going to lead multitudes to Christ as Savior. I saw that he was going to be successful largely because of her influence. I saw her as a mother of four children who were also going to be highly used of God to change the world. I saw that she was going to be very close to the Lord, happy and contented in life despite facing some difficult times. As I began to share this with her, I couldn't help but weep. I told her three times as I shared what I had seen of her future life, "Don't settle for anything less. Don't settle for anything less. Don't settle for anything less." I was wrecked by the amazing life that Father had planned for this girl. However, she didn't look surprised or different after receiving this word. It took me a few minutes to gather myself and minister to the remaining people. Ministry went on for probably another hour.

At the very end of the meeting as we were packing up to leave, the girl's parents came up to me and said, "We think that you need to know that she has been telling us for several days. The Lord has spoken to her that she is going to marry a man with a worldwide ministry and that he will lead multitudes to Christ and that she is going to have children that will change the world. Brother Roger, she also told us that the Lord said to her three times, 'Don't settle for anything less.'" It was very encouraging to know that I had gotten this word of wisdom correctly.

After this meeting, I was driving home and every time I would think of what the Lord had shown me about this girl's future, I would have to pull over because tears would come strongly. After the third or fourth time I pulled over, the Lord said to me, "Why are you reacting in this way? Don't you know that I have a wonderful plan for everyone, just like this girl?"

The Healing of a Ballerina

I was ministering in several churches in a particular region of the USA over a weekend. On Sunday morning, after I had preached the Good News and some had received healing, a young ballerina presented herself to me. I would guess that she was no more than 25 years old. She had damaged her right foot in a fall. I believe that she told me that she had gone through two operations to fix the problem but still had too much pain in the foot to be able to dance.

Until she heard me preach the Good News, she had believed that perhaps the Lord was trying to redirect her into another profession by the injury. She had heard me teach that God does not use sickness to teach us or guide us. Teaching us and guiding us is the work of the Holy Spirit. This helped her deal with this doubt and she was able to come for healing ministry believing that Jesus would heal her.

I had her sit in a chair and I knelt down and put my hands on her right foot. I felt a little bit of heat. I had her try the foot to see if there had been any change. She tried it and said, "It still hurts." So I had her sit down again. I prayed a second time and again felt just a little bit of heat. I had her try the foot again. This time she said, "It feels better but still hurts a little." I had her sit down for a third time and I prayed again for the foot. Again, I felt just a little bit of heat. I got her to try it again. This time, she was more enthusiastic and said, "It doesn't hurt but it really feels stiff." I had her sit again for a fourth time. I prayed again for her foot. Again, I felt just a little heat. I got her to stand up and try the foot again. This time, she started dancing and did not stop for more than a half an hour. She appeared to be crying the whole time.

I had gone back to praying for people and she came up and hugged me. She told me that she never wanted to do anything else but dance. She had spent her teenage years training to be a ballerina. When the injury had happened, she had come to believe that God did not wish her to be a ballerina and it broke her heart. She was depressed and discouraged. Now she saw that Father did approve of her desire to dance. Father had given her back her dream and her heart's desire.

Seeing a Baseball in the Spirit

I was preaching Christ as Healer and ministering to the sick in a church in Arizona. There had been many people healed. A man and a woman - who were both very large physically and appeared to be physically fit - approached me. They were dressed very nicely with what appeared to be very expensive clothing. The man said that he wanted prayer for a heart problem. I am six feet tall but I had to reach up to my head level to pray for this man's heart.

Nothing much seemed to be happening as I ministered to him. However, I glanced down at his hands and saw a baseball in his hand in the Spirit. (It wasn't actually there but a vision was imposed upon his hand.) I said to him, "Sir, are you a baseball coach?" With a surprised look, he said, "Yes." I asked him further, "Sir, are you considering leaving the coaching profession because you have a bad heart?" He said, "Yes" to me again. I said, "Sir, you can't leave the coaching profession; God called you to coaching. Coaching is your gift and ministry."

He and his wife began to cry, and healing flowed very strongly to his heart. He was completely healed at that time. Later, he told that he had wondered if God was trying to get him to leave coaching because he had a heart problem. This idea had created doubt for him. The word of knowledge about him being a baseball coach had removed the doubt and he was able to receive. I told him that God does not use sickness to guide us. He uses the Holy Spirit to guide us.

A Word of Knowledge About Serious Money

I was ministering in a large church in Toronto at a conference. We were seeing lots of healing and lots of excited Christian people as a result. One of the healing services came to an end so I was leaving and going back to my room. The sanctuary still had a lot of people in it.

Christians in this church are used to lingering, sitting and lying on the carpet and praying for each other long after the "formal" services are over with. As I went towards the door, quite a few people rose to their feet and held out their hands. This meant that they wanted me to touch their hands so that they would function in healing and miracles. They wanted an "impartation." I think that wanting to function in healing and miracles is a good thing, so I accommodated them by lightly slapping each hand extended to me as I left the building.

I had probably done this with 30 or more people when something different happened. I lightly slapped a young married woman's hands and immediate had a vision. It lasted for no more than two seconds. I saw - in the Spirit - a very large pile of money. I stopped immediately in front of her and spoke with her. I asked her if she had been praying for money. She said, "No." I then said to her, "Well, I think that you should do that. In fact, I think that you ought to ask the Lord for serious money." She said that she would do that. I slapped a few more hands and left the building.

Two weeks later, I got an email from her. She reminded me of what I had told her to do. She said that just as soon and she and her husband got back to their hotel room, they knelt down and prayed, "Lord Jesus, on the basis of the word that Roger Sapp gave us, we ask for serious money."

She said that in the next week her father had called her. He had been "day-trading" on the Stock Market and had made an amazing amount of money that week. Her father told her that he wanted to pay off the mortgage on their new home. He did that the very next day. She wrote, "That was very serious money."

A Man With Mixed Motives Healed

A Christian leader from a city that was a full day's drive from me called and asked me if I would meet with a man in his church who had environmental disease - chemical sensitivity - and minister healing to him. While I think that doing healing ministry by appointment is not the best way to do it, I agreed to meet with this man.

In a meeting, there is an expectation of hearing the Good News and we show that the will of God is to heal by doing a demonstration. A demonstration is getting someone up who has some sort of problem such as a bad back, difficulty walking, or something that is visibly wrong with them. We minister to them, and they receive a healing and are able to do things that they could not do before. This creates a stronger atmosphere of faith in Christ to help everyone receive.

Doing healing ministry by appointment doesn't allow me to build an atmosphere of faith in Christ by using the Good News and demonstrations. Nevertheless, I had made the appointment anyway, acknowledging that Jesus did heal a minority of people outside of the mass meetings where He preached the Good News and ministered to the multitudes.

So later in the week, according to the time of the appointment, this man arrived at my home. He was in his mid-thirties. He looked pale and seemed to be carrying a lot of stress. My initial impression of him, beyond his appearance, was that he was in a hurry. He seemed to want to get this over with and go about his business. I sat him down at the kitchen table and offered him something to drink. He declined the offered drink with a grimace as if the idea disgusted him. Because he asked me later about the water, I think that he was concerned about the purity of our water supply.

He was also highly agitated - with his eyes flitting around the room - and never making eye contact with me. As I tried to share some of the basics of the Good News with him, he kept interrupting me with questions about the house, such as: "What soap do you use to clean the kitchen? What fabric is the table cloth made from?" At one point, he asked to use the toilet and came back concerned about the toilet paper. All these questions did point to his real concern about exposure to chemicals. There was no doubt in my mind about this. I thought maybe that my impression of him being in a hurry was due to his fear of exposure to chemicals in my house.

After I determined that I had sufficiently shared the Good News with him, I asked him if he had any questions before he received healing from this condition. He said, "No." Because he was so distracted, I asked him to repeat back to me what I had told him. What I heard from him was pretty good. He did seem to understand the basics of the Good News. This was not too hard to understand since I knew that he attended a pretty good church with a good leader who was Christ-centered and kept the Good News at the center of his message every week.

I don't have any doubt that God does heal people of environmental disease without difficulties. I have seen people who are seriously ill, from exposure to a toxic substance, receive healing. I have seen people with serious chemical sensitivity be completely healed in our meetings. It really doesn't matter how they developed the problem for them to receive a healing by faith in Jesus Christ. Nothing is too hard for the Lord. Nothing is out of reach for those who believe in Him.

So then, I was ready to minister healing to him. I had him confess, "This healing belongs to me because of what Jesus has done." When I laid my hands on him, I had the "empty" feeling in my hands. This is one way that God guides people in healing ministry. This is different than just not feeling anything change in the hands. This "empty" feeling in my hands always means that someone is double-minded and wants to remain sick for some reason. It also means that there is no point praying until there is a change in the person. The Lord will not override the will of someone who doesn't want to be healed. However, just to make sure that I was getting it right, I went through the whole thing with him again and the "empty" feeling was strongly present again.

So with this information coming from revelation, I decided that I needed more information in this situation in order to help him. So I shifted back to talking with him to acquire facts. I asked him how long he had the problem with chemical sensitivity. If I remember correctly, he was 25 years old when he developed the problem. He had been disabled by it for a decade. I asked him if anything in particular happened to him to expose him to chemicals or make him sensitive to them before he developed the problem. He didn't have anything particular to tell me.

Then I asked him if anything tragic had happened to him just before he started developing chemical sensitivity. He reacted strongly to this question and wanted to leave immediately. I saw that this was a demonic reaction. He was much more agitated that I had seen him before. I convinced him to stay and in the next few minutes, a number of manipulative statements came out of him including the very common one that I have heard many times: "If you really knew how sick I am, you would not say this to me." When you hear this statement from someone that is ill, you can be fairly sure that they are using sickness to manipulate other people.

People who are using sickness for achieve something that they want, desire strongly to control what you think about them. If they cannot manipulate you, then they will shift to accusing you of being unkind or of being judgmental to control you. He did this to me and had a demonic manifestation happening as well. He clinched his jaw and ground his teeth as he was talking to me. I kept asking him what had happened to him just before developing chemical sensitivity. I reaffirmed to him that I believed that he was sensitive to chemicals, However, in order for him to be healed, he had to want it completely, and not want to remain sick for any reason.

Since he had come to me for help, I felt that I had complete permission to do what was necessary to help him. I waited for him to calm down and excused myself for a few minutes. I called the senior leader of his church who had made the original appointment with me. I told him what I suspected about this man. He told me that he was fairly sure that I was right but didn't know what had happened to him before he started developing this sensitivity.

I asked the senior leader to call the man's wife and tell her what we both suspected and ask her if she knew of any tragedy that had occurred before he started developing this chemical sensitivity. I went back in to where he was sitting at the table and had the phone with me. I told him that I was asking for some help to get him healed from people who knew him. He became agitated again and would not speak to me but didn't try to leave.

I fixed a cup of tea for him and for me and waited for a call back. (I didn't believe that he would drink the tea.) The senior leader called me back less than 15 minutes from the time that I had talked with him. He told me that this man's wife had told him of a horrible event in his work situation that had completely devastated him. The wife also suspected that it was a key element in his illness. The senior leader did not tell me what the event was but indicated that it would be extremely embarrassing to any man for something like this to be public knowledge. He had never tried to go back to work since then. In other words, he developed the chemical sensitivity after he had chosen not to work. It had given him something to point to as the reason that he could not work. Despite the fact that he did have chemical sensitivity, it was not the real reason why he didn't want to work.

I told him that I knew that there was an extremely painful event that made him choose not to work, and that he needed to face this issue and determine that he could not spend the rest of his life avoiding this. I also told him that the chemical sensitivity could be healed by the Lord, and that the Lord could take away this emotional pain, but he had to no longer excuse himself from working. He was no longer aggressive with me and no longer agitated. He made what appeared to me to be a weak commitment to getting well and doing the right thing. It was apparently enough for the Lord. When I laid hands on him this time, lots of deliverance from demons occurred and heat flowed in healing to him. He walked out of the house a new man.

I talked with the senior leader of his church several weeks later, and things were going pretty well with this man. He had no trace of chemical sensitivity and was publically declaring himself healed. He had also applied for several jobs.

This was somewhat short-lived, however. In a few more weeks, the senior leader called me with him on the phone line. The man (who had been healed) complained to me that the chemical sensitivity had returned. I asked him about how his job hunt was going. When I brought this up, he tried to manipulate me by saying, "If you only knew how bad I feel, you wouldn't ask me about having a job."

I questioned him and discovered what had happened. When he didn't get a job at the first two places that he applied, he had quit applying. This minor disappointment caused him to go back to being double-minded, and that allowed the symptoms of chemical sensitivity to return. He wanted an excuse not to work and the devil was willing to give him one.

The senior leader and I reaffirmed to him that the will of God was for him to be well and to be employed. I talked with him about being careful about wanting not to work, and not to try to escape this responsibility through illness.

I had this same conversation with him at least four times in the next year. He would slide back into wanting to excuse himself though illness when he was discouraged.

I found out that before he had met me, his wife had told him the truth about why he was sick. She wouldn't let it go despite his attempts to manipulate her. The reason that he had come to my house originally was to prove her wrong. He would have me pray for him to prove to her that he wanted to be healed, but he had no intentions or expectations of being healed. In other words, his trip to see me was entirely for the purpose of manipulating her. (The Lord had a much better plan for him.)

He did finally get a job and struggled with working at first but the senior leader set up a group of men to keep him on track. Successfully working through difficulties on the job seemed to rebuild his self-esteem. Additionally, the positive reactions of his wife to him being employed all seemed to help him not become double-minded again.

I hope that everyone remembers that the great majority of Christians who are unhealed are not choosing to remain that way. It is only 1% of unhealed Christians that may be double-minded about sickness and healing.

"But when he asks, he must believe and not doubt, because he who doubts is like a wave of the sea, blown and tossed by the wind. That man should not think he will receive anything from the Lord; he is a double-minded man, unstable in all he does." (James 1:6-8)

Doubting is disqualifying yourself from being healed. Most believers who are disqualifying themselves are doing it unintentionally. However, a small percentage of Christians make a decision to remain sick. They are not 100% committed to this decision but are not 100% committed to receiving a healing either. They have mixed motives. They are double-minded. While in this unwholesome condition, they will not receive anything from the Lord.

The Ball of Fire

I was teaching on Christ-centered healing during a Sunday service at a church. As I taught and was looking out at the audience, a small ball of fire - about the size of a ping-pong ball - appeared above a young woman's head who was sitting in the second or third row. The ball of fire then dropped and disappeared into her head. I stopped teaching, pointed to her and said, "The young woman in the blue dress. What are you feeling?" She said, "My head feels hot." Just as she said this, words came into my consciousness, "Learning disability." I said, "The Lord has just healed you of a learning disability." She said, "I have dyslexia and have trouble reading." I said, "Not anymore." From that moment on, she had no trouble reading. The dyslexia was completely gone. Jesus had healed her.

The Healing of Cancer in a Young Man

We had a Tuesday night meeting where I would teach a Christ-centered message on receiving and ministering healing. After I would teach, the entire group would minister to those who wanted to receive healing ministry. On one Tuesday evening, a young man came who was very sick with cancer. He was also suffering from nausea because he had taken chemotherapy that day. He was diagnosed with two large cancerous tumors. One tumor was under his ribs and one in his hip. His facial color was gray from the chemotherapy. We laid hands on him and within moments, his color changed to pink and he was warm all over. The nausea was completely gone and we were fairly sure that he was healed. He went back to his doctor in a few days and after some x-rays, his doctor said - in amazement - that one of the tumors was completely gone and the other was half the size that it was previously. After a second time of ministry with him, he was completely free from cancer. Now, keep in mind that this man was under medical care both before and after his healing. Obviously, Father did not require him to refuse medical care in order to be healed.

Blind Woman Sees Flags

I was ministering in a fellowship of believers in a southern state in the USA. The leader's mother was present. I am guessing that she was in her 60's. She had gone blind due to the effect of diabetes, if I remember correctly. She presented herself for ministry after hearing the Good News about what Jesus had done for her. The irises in both her eyes had lost color. Her eyes were very white. I had her face the people watching, and laid hands on her with my index fingers lightly touching her eyelids. I felt some heat and then had her look at me. A brown color had partially returned to her eyes. There was an excited acknowledgement in the church that her eyes were very different than before. She was still not seeing but said that she could see more light.

I did the same thing again with my index fingers lightly touching her eyelids. I had her open her eyes again. This time, her eyes looked a very normal color; a dark brown. I asked her to look at the back of the church and read the sign above the doorway. She said, "You mean the one that says 'Exit'?" The entire church started laughing. I asked her to tell me the color of the flags that were displayed across the back of the church from left to right. She started calling out colors but they were not the colors of the flags. For a moment I was puzzled, but then I realized that she was calling out the colors - backwards - from right to left. She was completely healed. Thank you, Lord Jesus.

My Wife Healed in Shopping Mall

My wife Ann and I were walking in a mall and talking. I don't believe that we were talking about anything particularly spiritual, but I guess when a married couple talks with each other, it is spiritual in itself. I had my left arm around her touching her shoulders and neck. Without any warning, I felt healing flow to the back of her neck and shoulders. I had felt this happen many times in healing ministry but it rarely happened outside of the circumstance of actually praying for healing for someone.

I stopped walking and, following my lead, she stopped also. I said, "I just felt healing flow to you. Are you okay?" She said, "Well, my neck and shoulders have felt very tight and I have a little bit of a headache." I said, "How is it now?" She moved her shoulders around and then moved her neck from side to side. She said, "Actually, my shoulders and neck feel much more relaxed." I said, "What about the headache?" She stopped moving and looked upward for a moment. She then said, "It seems to be gone."

I said to her jokingly, "Why didn't you tell me that you were not feeling good? You do know that I am involved in healing ministry?" She and I laughed. Then she said, "I did tell the Lord that I was not feeling well."

When she said this, I saw what had happened. She had come to Christ her Healer in simple faith that He would help her. Christ in me had answered her prayer by healing her. The thing that was pretty amazing about this was the fact that I was not involved in this healing even though it had come through me. The reality of Christ and

72

His ongoing involvement with us was so clear at that moment.

Since that time, I have had a few more experiences like this one. For instance, on several occasions when I entered a meeting of God's people for the first time, someone would stick out their hand to greet me. I would shake their hand and feel healing flow to them. I would ask them if they were expecting to receive a healing at this meeting and they would say "Yes." I would then tell them that I think that they just received their healing and if there was a way to check it out to do so. Once in a while, someone will testify to being healed in this way. Thank you, Jesus.

Healing Evangelist Healed of Cancer

A woman friend of mine called me by telephone to ask if I would pray - by phone - for another friend of hers who had terminal cancer. He was an evangelist who often saw people healed in his ministry. He was in hospice and not expected to live much longer. I dislike doing telephone ministry and seldom agree to it. I have good reasons for this. I much prefer to thoroughly preach the Good News before ministering to people. The percentages of people receiving healing seem much higher in an environment charged with the Good News. They receive healing more quickly and much easier as well. Often, they receive healing - without anyone praying for them - as they soak in the Good News about what Jesus has done for them. However, because this man had much previous experience with healing, I responded favorably to my woman friend's request.

I got this man on the telephone. I told him that I wanted to speak to him about what Jesus had done for him in regard to healing. I told him that I understood that he already knew these things, but I wanted to bring the Good News to him because Christ had set that pattern. The great majority of Christ's healings came as the multitudes came to Him after He had preached to them the Good News.

To his credit, this Christian minister said for me not to be concerned that he already knew these things. He said that he would probably do the same thing if the roles were reversed. I then spent a few minutes outlining for him the Good News and exactly why the Lord was going to heal him. I then prayed with him over the phone and had him make the confession, "This healing belongs to me because of what Jesus has done." He did this and shortly we ended the conversation.

About two weeks later, my woman friend called me and asked if I had heard the story about this man. I told her that I had not heard anything. She said to me that shortly after our conversation that he had gotten very hot. The nurses in the hospice were concerned that he had gotten an infection and gave him medications to bring down his fever. They had not worked. He remained hot for three days even while he slept. At the end of the three days, he was strong and no longer had cancer. He was released from hospice care. He had received a "cleansing" from the Lord. He had been purged of cancer. Thank you, Lord.

Blind Woman Healed

Not long ago, I was invited to a nation in Asia to preach Christ as Healer. I had a male friend travel with me. He was trained in our ministry a number of years ago and has healing working very well. On a particular weekend, we were ministering in a small church.

On Friday night, I prayed for a woman who was completely blind. She saw nothing but black. She had no perception of light. After prayer, she confessed to seeing light. Everything that was previously black was now white. I asked her to return on Saturday to hear the Good News again and to receive prayer.

She returned on Saturday, and heard the Good News again. My traveling companion prayed with her. She began seeing but in an unusual way. She should see clearly from the middle of her vision downward. However, she could only see white above the middle of her vision. He asked her to return on Sunday to hear the Good News and receive prayer again. She was encouraged and very willing to do this.

She returned on Sunday, heard the Good News and received prayer from both my traveling companion and myself. The top of her vision cleared and she was able to see normally. Jesus had completely healed her. Thank you, Lord.

Word of Knowledge that Came as a Vision

I was ministering healing in a church west of where we live in Texas. We were having a productive meeting with many people being healed. In fact, the senior leader later told me in writing that he had a least a hundred healing testimonies in a three-hundred-member fellowship. While I was ministering, a man came forward for healing ministry and when I laid my hands on him, I immediately saw him standing in a dry cleaners. This was happening with most of the church looking on and hearing what I was saying over the sound system.

This particular word of knowledge came in the form of a vision of him standing in a dry cleaners. I told him what I was seeing and asked him if it meant anything to him. He said, "No." I said, "Okay, but I believe that this will come to mean something to you." I continued to minister to him, and within another minute, I again saw really clearly him standing in a dry cleaners. Again I asked him, "Are you sure that standing in a dry cleaners doesn't mean anything to you?" Again, he said, "No, it doesn't mean anything to me." Well, I went on with ministry to him and he did seem to receive the healing that he was expecting.

Probably ten minutes had passed and I was ministering to the next person waiting for me. The man that I had seen standing in a dry cleaners interrupted me. He held up a piece of paper and said, "See that woman sitting in the back of the church?" (She waved at me.) I said, "Yes, I see her." He said, "Well, I own an empty building downtown. She wants to rent it from me and turn it into a dry cleaners. She just asked me and presented me this contract. Do you think that I ought to do this?" He laughed and the whole church broke up laughing. God has a wonderful sense of humor, even when He is guiding His people.

Spiritual Treasure
44 True Stories of the Supernatural Grace of God

A "Crazy" Woman Healed and Delivered

As I have repeatedly written, an estimated 1% of the unhealed Christians in the Church are mixed in motives. They may want healing but also want to remain sick for other reasons. Now, I am not talking about faking an illness. They are really ill but don't receive healing because of mixed motives. Staying sick allows some of these people to avoid working. There are probably multiple explanations for why a person doesn't want to work, but a major one is simple laziness.

A few years ago, I worked with a Christian half-way house. It was full of new converts, some from drug addiction and some from alcohol addiction. They all lived together in a large house and counselors lived there also. I got a call about a woman in the house who was occasionally "crazy' and violent. She would hiss and roar at people, grab objects, break them or throw them at people, scratch, bite, and hit people in the face with her fist. She was a convert out of drug addiction and prostitution. She had gotten arrested, convicted, and was on probation. The courts had also declared her an unfit mother and had put her two children in foster care. Her motive for accepting Christ and getting clean was that she wanted her children back.

They asked me if I would do deliverance with her. My response was "When does she go crazy? What sets her off?" They said it was almost always when they asked her to do her share of the chores in the house. However, they had quit asking her to help because they had become afraid of her.

When she arrived at my location with one of the woman counselors, it was clear that she didn't want to be there. When I prayed initially for her, there was no presence of the Holy Spirit to help her. This always means that the person is double-minded and really doesn't want help or to change at some level.

I confronted her with not being willing to work. She immediately stood up and started doing the violent "crazy" thing. She first of all tried to get to my fireplace where there were some expensive sculptures. I blocked her way, and then she came at me with a wild look in her eye. I said, "Being crazy is sure to keep you from getting your children back." She immediately calmed down.

I then told her that she was lazy and irresponsible and that had to change for her to be a fit mother. The fact that she would not do her share of the work proved that she was still unfit. The fact that she would frighten people to keep from working also proved she was unfit. I also said to her that because she was lazy and irresponsible, she would go back to a wicked life of easy money through prostitution and drug addiction. She needed to repent deeply of these things. Thankfully, her desire to get her children back was strong enough to plow through self-righteousness and justifications for remaining as she was. She repented and was no longer double-minded. Her deliverance from evil spirits flowed strongly for several hours. She was a new woman afterward. The counselors told me that they could not believe the change.

However, after a few months had passed, she went back to her old ways and ended up on my doorstep again. Again, there was no presence of the Holy Spirit to help her. She was double-minded again. She didn't like being responsible. She didn't like working. She wanted to be lazy. She had already moved back towards the lifestyle of prostitution. The counselors were pretty certain that she had taken money for sex in the past few weeks. They were certain that she was "high" - intoxicated by drugs - occasionally. I confronted her again and immediately she was "crazy", but just as soon as I saw that I said, "Being crazy will not help you get your children back. Only being responsible will do that." "Crazy" disappeared immediately. She broke down and cried, saying that it was hard to be responsible but that she would try again. Deliverance flowed with ease with her again.

The last that I heard about her is that she was walking victoriously with the Lord and that she had gotten her children back. There is always power in the Spirit to help people who want help. However, the Holy Spirit will not violate the will of people. If they want something else, He will allow them to have it. It is important, therefore, for all believers to make firm choices to do the right thing. The Holy Spirit will acknowledge those choices and empower us to live righteously.

Healing of a Gold Toe

I was invited to minister healing at a church in a community a few miles north of Dallas, Texas. I had preached there on Friday evening and there were quite a few that were healed. It was now Sunday, and the pastor asked me if I could come to the church an hour before the service started to pray with him and the leadership for the morning service. I arrived at the building an hour early and when I walked into the front door, I immediately began to see a man's right foot whose big toe looked seriously damaged. It was black and blue. No matter where I looked, this image was imposed on everything. It is a little hard to describe. I would see everything that I was looking at, but see this as well. I went to prayer with the leaders and the vision remained.

The service started and the vision remained all through worship which lasted an hour. Everywhere I looked, I saw this foot with the damaged big toe. I decided that after I preached, I would give this information about the damaged toe as a word of knowledge. However, when I got up to preach the service, the image intensified as I attempted to preach Christ the Healer. The image became so strong that I was having trouble seeing anything else. I yielded to this because I believed it was the Lord saying to me, "Share it now." So I said to the congregation, "I intended to preach Jesus Christ the Healer to you and perhaps that will happen, but right now the Lord wants me to stop and tell you this." I then proceeded to tell the congregation what I had been seeing for the past two hours.

Spiritual Treasure
44 True Stories of the Supernatural Grace of God

There was a shout of "Hallelujah" and a man in the front row started moving towards me somewhat hindered by the fact that he was taking his shoe and sock off of his right foot. When he arrived at the podium, I came out to meet him and asked him, "What is happening with you?" He pointed down at his big toe on his right foot. It was painted gold. He said, "You see that my big toe is painted gold?" I said, "Yes, I see that. Why is it painted gold?" He said that he was a construction worker and decided because his feet were bothering him to wear some soft shoes to work rather than his safety shoes. He got away with this for several days and it did seem to help his feet feel better. However, as he continued wearing more comfortable shoes, he eventually dropped a heavy cinderblock and one of the corners of the cinderblock landed directly on his big toe.

He was in great pain and could hardly walk afterward. The impact had crushed the bones in his toe. It had also broken the skin in several places and created a lot of bleeding. His shoe became full of blood. He left work and called back that he was feeling bad - which was true - and needed to take a day of sick leave. He was afraid to report it because it was against the rules not to wear safety shoes. He decided to believe the Lord for his healing. However, after a week or so, the toe started looking much worse. It was infected and was much larger than normal. It was also giving him a great deal of pain when he walked on it. He said, "Every time I felt pain, I would claim my healing. However, when I looked at the big toe, it looked increasingly worse and I was gripped by fear that I was getting gangrene and might even lose the foot. Looking at the foot completely disrupted my faith, so I decided to paint it gold to cover up the ugly colors to remind myself that Jesus was healing it. It has been painted gold for just about a day and since I knew that I was coming to this healing service, I was expecting the Lord to heal me."

I knelt down and confessed healing over the gold toe because of what Jesus had done. A strong flow of heat came and he confessed to feeling like his toe was "cooking." The toe was healed within two minutes or so. He said it felt great. I asked him to test the toe by walking and putting pressure on it. He walked without pain. He pressed hard on the toe without pain. I asked him to remove the paint if he could. Some people brought him water and soap from the bathroom and one woman gave him some nail polish remover. He had our attention as he removed the paint. As a result of the toe looking completely normal, he started crying.

There was a strong flow of the word of knowledge at that point. I revealed specifics on several other healing issues. The people that responded to those revelations received healing. I made the point repeatedly that you do not have to have a word of knowledge in order to receive a healing. I never got to preach that Sunday. The "gold toe" was the message that day. The pastor told me that he estimated that 70 people of his 120-plus congregation received healing that day. There was also a very unusual healing of cancer at the very end of the service. It is the next story in this book.

Dying Man Healed of Cancer

As a result of the healing of the "gold toe," we had a lot of healing happen for several hours after this Sunday morning service in a church north of Dallas, Texas. The service began to wind down and most of the people had gone. The senior pastoral leader of this church and I were standing up at the front of the church where we had been praying for healing but had reached a time when no one was coming any more for ministry.

So we were just talking with one another about what had happened in that service and waiting to see if anyone else was going to come for ministry. We saw a woman come in the back of the church with a man who looked like he was ill. She had her arm around him and they walked slowly up to the front of the church where we were standing. He was pale and my first thought was, "This man has the flu." This was because influenza was common in the region at that time. Many people were sick with it.

The woman said to us, "My husband has been ill and he doesn't speak English. He only speaks Spanish. Would you pray for his healing? I will translate." I said, "Of course, we will pray for his healing." The pastor and I laid hands on him and within a few seconds, I felt him get extremely hot. In fact, he was radiating heat from all over his body. He was receiving a cleansing.

I said to the woman, "Ask him what he is feeling." She asked him in Spanish what he was feeling, and he replied to her in Spanish. She told us that he was feeling very hot. I said to her, "Tell him that I think that he is healed."

The man seemed to agree and did look better and certainly acted stronger. They left the church and the pastor and I concluded that we were done, and shortly afterward I left to return home.

Several days later, the pastor called me to report on this situation. What had happened was that his wife had been in the earlier service. She had seen the man with the gold toe receive healing and had seen many other people receive healing. Her husband was in hospice care because he was dying of brain cancer, and the cancer had spread throughout his body. He was not expected to live more than a few weeks. When she had seen so many people receive healing, she decided to go get her husband and bring him to the service. When she arrived at the hospice, the people on the staff resisted her taking her husband, but she insisted. They could not legally resist her wishes. She even pulled a morphine IV drip out of his arm and got him dressed against the wishes of the staff. All the time, she was praying for the service to last long enough for her to get back with him so that we could minister to him.

He was completely healed of cancer. The pastor went on to tell me on the phone that because of this healing, more than ten members of his family had received Christ as Savior already and he expected more family members to receive Christ soon. They all knew that he was dying and then suddenly he was well. This story of his healing by Jesus Christ had spread through the entire Hispanic community and many were asking questions about exactly what had happened.

Dying Woman in the ICU Healed of Cancer

A few years back, a Dallas pastor whom I didn't know called me. He asked me to pray for a 30-year-old woman, a member of his congregation, who was in a Dallas hospital. She was very ill with cancer and they did not expect her to live much longer. She had recently become unconscious and they had to take her off the IV that was both feeding her and providing her water. This was because her kidneys had quit functioning. If fluid from an IV continues to flow into a person that no longer has the ability to remove fluid from their body, they will blow up with fluid and this can cause their death. My wife is a Registered Nurse and she has told me that when a patient's kidneys quit functioning and they are not regaining consciousness that it means they will likely die within 72 hours.

I called two men that I had been training in healing ministry and asked them to come with me to pray for her the next day. We met for breakfast that day and then went to the hospital. Her family was present and obviously expecting her to die. The pastor was present and he introduced us to the family. He stayed with the family and the three of us went into the Intensive Care Unit to her bed. There were nurses coming and going but there was not much more they could do for her.

I stood by her bed with these two other men and quietly spoke the Good News about what Jesus had done for her. I told her why I believed that she would be healed when I laid my hands on her. I told her that Jesus had revealed the will of the Father by healing all who had come to Him. I spoke briefly about what the cross had accomplished. This lasted probably no more than 5 minutes. Because I was speaking quietly, several nurses stopped to listen. If you want people to strain to listen, speak quietly. If you want someone to react negatively, be offended, and not listen, talk loudly.

Some might wonder why I would do this with an unconscious woman. Could she hear this? I am not certain, but I could hear it. My two friends could hear it. The nurses coming and going could hear it. The angels of God could hear it. The demons could hear it. The vast majority of the healings of Jesus Christ came after He had preached the Good News, and the New Testament says that "Faith comes by hearing and hearing by the word of Christ." This is why I did it. The Good News changes everything for the better.

I laid hands on her and felt almost immediately a tiny trickle of electricity go into her. This felt much like static electricity except there was no pop. It just flowed into her. I sensed that we were done and we left the ICU, then left without interacting with either the pastor or the family.

The pastor called me later that week and said that during the night, her kidneys began to function. She became conscious shortly thereafter. The next morning she showed no sign of sickness. They checked her for cancer and did not find any. She left the hospital a day later completely well. I rejoiced with him over this but I never heard from him again. I guess that he didn't have anyone 'se in his congregation that was sick or was ever going be sick. I would have been glad to come preach Christ Healer to his congregation.

Healing of a Witch

I was doing healing meetings in another country for a few weeks. At one of the meetings, the leader who had invited me and had sponsored these meetings approached me. He said, "Roger, do you see the four people who have just come into the back of the building?" I said, "Yes." There were three women and a man. He said, "They are four well-known witches in our area. The woman on the far left is very well-known for her ability to channel spirits for supernatural guidance to the businessmen in our area. What do you want to do about this?" I said, "Nothing at all. I can't think of a better place for them to be."

The meeting seemed to go well. I preached the Good News about Christ as Healer. In situations like this, I most often do a "demonstration." I ask for someone who is ready to be healed and has a bad back, a bad shoulder, or arm that they cannot raise, or perhaps bad knees to come forward and allow me to minister healing to them. We do a "before and after" with them. We evaluate- before praying for them - how serious their problem is. Then we minister to them and have them do things that they couldn't do before. This provides a very visible change for the audience to see that they are healed. It increases expectation in the audience of them receiving healing as well.

I had reached the point of demonstration. I explained why I wanted someone who was injured to come forward. Without hesitation, the witch who channeled spirits came forward. I interviewed her and she did have a painful back injury. She could not bend very far before she was in serious pain. She said that she took pain medication for it. She said despite the medication, she often had trouble sleeping because of pain.

I put my hands on her lower back and had her say, "This healing belongs to me because of what Jesus has done." She made the confession. Very quickly, a strong presence of heat came to her back. Within moments, I was sure that she was healed. I got her to bend and test the healing. She went all the way down and touched her toes. She came up sobbing and thanking the Lord. She was completely healed. By the end of the week, she and her three friends - witches before - had received Christ as Savior. Thank you, Jesus.

When telling this story, I often ask the audience if she was a believer. The vast majority of the people will say "No." Then I will say to them "I didn't ask if she was a Christian. I asked if she was a believer. She heard the Good News. She responded in simple faith to the idea that Christ would heal her. She demonstrated that faith by coming forward and letting me minister to her. Was she a believer in the same sense that the multitudes were who came to Christ for healing?" Then everyone will agree that she was a believer in that sense. I will then ask, "Who do you think receives healing--believers or Christians? There are many Christians that do not actively believe that Christ is their Healer. However, there are many unsaved persons - engaged in sin of various types - that will actively believe in Christ as Healer when they hear the Good News." We should not be afraid to tell witches that Jesus will heal them. They may be much more open to this than we would assume. Beyond that, converted witches often make excellent Christians as they will not be satisfied with sitting in the pew. They will want to experience all that God has for them.

Martial Artist with Cancer Healed

At the end of several weeks of healing ministry in another country, I was preaching a message with a particular theme about Christ healing imperfect people. There were many people receiving healing from the Lord.

A Christian couple had driven six hours to pick up a friend who was dying of cancer. He was unable to get to the meeting on his own because he was too sick. He had brain cancer. It had spread to the tissue behind his eyes. He was experiencing bleeding into his throat that choked him. Additionally, he was experiencing a good deal of pain and taking some heavy painkillers to deal with it. He had been told that his cancer was terminal and that soon, he would have to go to hospice.

This man responded to my message by saying to himself, "If Christ is healing imperfect people, I qualify." He and his friends came forward to me and asked for prayer for him. They explained to me that he had cancer behind his eyes. This man, of Chinese heritage, allowed me to lay my hands on his forehead. I had him say the confession, "This healing belongs to me because of what Jesus has done." He did this and I felt some warmth enter his forehead. I asked him if he had felt this and he said, "Yes." I told him that I thought he was healed. He politely thanked me and left with his two friends.

His friends took him home after the meeting. Within that first hour of driving, the bloody discharge down this throat stopped. By the time he had arrived back home, he felt so good that he decided not to take his pain medication. He slept through the night without a problem for the first time for a long season.

The next morning, he made an appointment with his doctor who concluded in the next few days that he no longer had cancer. As a result of this, the man called the ministry headquarters and spoke to the leader's wife and told her of his healing. She rejoiced with him over this. During this conversation, he asked, "What was it that man had me say?" She said to him, "He had you say, 'This healing belongs to you because of what Jesus has done.'" He said to her, "What has Jesus done?" She explained to him that Jesus had died for both his sins and his sickness. He then prayed with her to receive Christ as his Savior.

Up to then, he was a practicing Buddhist. He was a man of good reputation and had done much for young people in his country. He was a high-ranking martial arts master and had many schools and students in his country. They knew that he was dying from cancer but then began to hear about his healing by Jesus and his acceptance of Christ as his Savior. The last we heard is that many of his students had become Christians as a result of his testimony.

Hell's Angel Healed

I was ministering in central Texas in a house church network. I preached Christ as Healer to a full house from the kitchen table. At the end of my message, I asked for someone who had a severe injury such as a bad back, a frozen shoulder, or bad knees to come forward to receive a healing in front of everyone. We call this a demonstration. It helps create a better atmosphere of faith in Christ if people see something visibly change in someone who needs healing. As a result, after preaching the Gospel of Christ as Healer, I often minister healing to someone who is injured in front of an audience of people seeking healing so that all can see the change happen when that person is healed.

In answer to my request for someone who was injured, a man wearing Hell's Angels motorcycle club's leather vest (called a "cut") responded. He had very long hair and a beard, if I remember correctly. He came forward with a severe limp and was using a cane. He explained that he had been wounded in the Vietnam War and for decades had not been able to walk very well. I laid hands on him and got him to do the confession, "This healing belongs to me because of what Jesus has done." As he did this, he was immediately healed and had no trouble walking. He walked very normally and tested the healing. The house seemed to buzz with excitement over this very visible healing and others were healed as well.

A couple of years later, I was attending a house church conference and saw my friends from this house church movement in central Texas. They pointed at a particular man - dressed in a suit and tie - and asked me if I remembered him. He was sitting in a chair and he grinned at me. He didn't look familiar. Then they told me that he was the Hell's Angel that had received healing. They told me that he had received Christ as Savior shortly afterward. He grinned at me again. I was able to greet him as my brother in Christ and rejoice over his salvation. Thank you, Jesus.

A Reluctant Man with a Bad Back Healed

A man with a very bad back came forward during a healing meeting as I was praying for the sick. He presented himself very reluctantly. His body language told me that he didn't want to be there. The way that he carried himself and the way that he was dressed also told me about him. Despite there being plenty of the presence and power of the Holy Spirit, when I laid hands on him, there was nothing. This usually happens when someone is double-minded about being healed.

I asked him, "Do you want to be healed?" He looked at me, turning his head slightly, and said, "Have you been talking to my wife?" I laughed and responded to this by saying, "No, what would she say to me about you wanting to be healed?" He didn't say anything. I said to him, "I am assuming that she would say that she thinks that you don't really want to be healed? Is that right?" He said, "Are you saying that I am not really disabled?" I responded, "No, I believe that you are disabled, but I also believe that you don't want to be healed for some reason. Is it because you don't want to work? Is this what your wife would say?" He said, "Yes, that is what she would say." I asked him, "Do you have children, and if so, what ages?" He said that he had two teenage boys. I asked him, "What do your boys think about you? Do they agree with your wife?" He said, "Yes, I think that they agree with my wife." Tell me why don't you want to work? His revealed a serious fear of failure. He had gotten fired from several jobs and his fragile self-image was not up the challenge of going back to work. Being disabled allowed him to excuse himself from facing the challenge of working. He didn't want to give that up.

I told him that in order to regain the respect of his wife and children, he had to face his fear. He had to be committed to receiving his healing and facing the future with courage. I told him that the Lord would help him.

The thought of losing or regaining the respect of their families is very powerful to men. It will often motivate them to do the right thing. In this case, this man confessed his fear to the Lord, repented of wanting to be sick and received a healing shortly afterward.

Since most of this happened in a relatively private situation between him, myself and the Lord in the church building, I asked his permission to talk with the leader of his church about helping him stay in the right place to retain his healing. He gave me permission and I discussed him and his situation with the leader.

A few months later, he and the leader got me on the phone because he was struggling with the fear again. I reminded him of what he was obtaining for himself by being courageous. He was obtaining the respect of his family. I asked him, "Haven't you felt better about yourself doing the right thing despite having some fears?" He admitted to me that he was feeling better about himself. We had one more talk in the next year. He was doing much better. He was able to maintain his healing. He regained his self-respect and the respect of his family.

By the way, a common characteristic of men who are using sickness in their lives to avoid working is that they look like they are carrying a thousand-pound load on their back. They do not often stand up straight. (This may be the effect of guilt.) They have trouble looking you in the eye. Often their clothes are worn out and they look as if personal grooming has not happened in a long time. Family members and often people in the church who know them well understand that they are sick but are using the sickness to get what they want. At the same time, they do not understand how to help them.

Again, I write this in order to help these people, not to condemn them in any way. Jesus wants to help them. I want to help them. Christian people who have some desire to remain sick does not describe the great majority of unhealed Christians. It only describes an estimated 1% of the Body of Christ.

Healing of a Deaf Girl

I was ministering in a large city in central USA. A preteen girl presented herself to me but didn't say anything. I asked her if I could pray for her and she didn't respond. However, her mother who was seated said, "Roger, she is 100% deaf. She became deaf from having Rheumatic Fever."

I said, "Oh, okay. That explains why she is not responding." I put my index fingers in both her ears and said, "This healing belongs to you because of what Jesus has done." I can't say that I felt a lot but people are often healed without me feeling much. Because of knowing this, I said to her, "Can you hear me?" She said, "Yes." without changing expressions.

Because of the ease of this healing and the fact of the girl not showing any excitement, I thought that I might have gotten the situation wrong. I looked at her mother and said, "You did say that she was entirely deaf?" Her mother said, "Yes, she is entirely deaf."

I looked back at the girl and said again, "Can you hear me?" She said, "Yes." again. I started to laugh because this healing came so easily that I had doubted that she had been totally deaf. I covered one of her ears and spoke to her and then covered the other ear and spoke to her. She could hear normally with both ears. Interestingly, the girl never changed expression. Perhaps this was because she completely believed that Jesus would heal her and she was not surprised when it happened.

Healing of a Hole in My Heart

On a Saturday morning while I was waiting for the pastor to pick me up for a healing teaching session, I was watching the news on the television. I started feeling a very mild headache and my vision started to change strangely. There appeared a black hole in the middle of my vision. Around the hole, things that I could see on the edges of my vision were swirling around, falling into the hole and disappearing.

My first thought about this was "I am having a stroke" so I began to pray for my own healing. I also thought that having a stroke in a hotel room -with no one else around - is a really bad idea. I got up and discovered that my balance was not good. I went to the telephone and tried to dial the lobby of the hotel but couldn't see the phone well enough to do this. I decided that my safest choice was to go to the lobby.

I left the room and because my balance was very bad, I held on to the wall all around to the lobby. When I arrived there, I told the people at the desk that I might be having a stroke and sat down on a chair. They immediately called emergency services and 10 minutes later, an ambulance and two emergency medical technicians arrived. However, by this time, the event had completely passed. I was no longer having a problem. I didn't have a mild headache any longer. I was seeing normally. Nevertheless, as a precaution, I decided to go to the hospital.

At the hospital emergency room, they did several tests on me to determine what had happened to me. They quickly ruled out a stroke or heart attack. There was no damage to my brain or heart. The emergency room physician told me that I had had a "TIA" and I needed to see my doctor about this as soon as I returned home.

A "TIA" is a transient ischemic attack. It is sometimes called a mini-stroke, with stroke symptoms that last less than 24 hours before disappearing. While a "TIA" generally doesn't cause permanent brain damage, it is a serious warning sign of stroke and should not be ignored.

When I got home, my doctor sent me to a specialist who - after many tests - finally diagnosed me with having a hole in my heart that allowed plaque to pass through and that was the cause of the TIA. He said that I had probably always had this hole, but it had gotten bigger. If I understand this correctly, plaque from my arteries had gotten in my eye and had interfered with the neurological signals from my eye to my brain.

This doctor told me that I was in great danger of having a stroke because this hole in my heart could also allow plaque to get to my brain and cause a stroke. He told me that I needed to consider surgery on my heart, but in the meantime, he gave me a handful of prescriptions for drugs such as blood thinners that would keep me from dying. I took the prescriptions but told him that I believed that Jesus would heal me. I decided that I would not fulfill the prescriptions before the next weekend. I wanted to give the Lord an opportunity to heal me. I received the prescriptions and diagnosis on Tuesday.

On Friday evening, at a church, I admitted to the audience that I was in need of healing myself. I intended

to preach Christ as Healer to them and then receive prayer after praying for all those who want to receive a healing. However, when I admitted this need - an evangelist that I had been training in healing ministry - immediately stood up and came over to me and laid his hands on my heart. That region of my chest became very hot and my heart was healed. Testing has shown that I no longer have this problem. It has been seven or eight years since this event and I have never had another TIA.
 Thank you, Lord.

The Metronome

Sometimes, words of knowledge come to me as visions. I was ministering in a church and received similar words of knowledge that involved two different women. I saw a hazy object in a young woman's hand. It was like a green pyramid but I wasn't seeing it clear enough to know what it was. So I asked the Lord what I was seeing but didn't get an answer immediately. I continued to minister healing to people coming for prayer.

About an hour later, I saw the same object in another woman's hand but this time, it was bright and clear. It was a green metronome, which is an instrument used to keep time as a musician. I said to her that I believed that she had a musical gift. The entire church broke up with laughter. She was an accomplished composer, a talented singer, and a professor of music in a local university. I laughed also.

I realized at that moment, that what I had seen in the young woman's hand was the same thing but being less clear and less bright meant that this gift was undeveloped. I pointed at the young woman that I previously ministered to and told her, "You also have a musical gift and it is not completely developed yet." She started crying and said, "I felt that the Lord was calling me to study music." I said, "I believe that He is." Our Father is very interested in His children knowing His gracious and perfect plan for their lives.

A Humorous Word of Knowledge

A few years back, when I would preach and stand for hours ministering healing to people, my feet would start to hurt. The longer I would stand, the more distracting the pain in my feet would be. As I would pray for healing of the pain of other people, I would be distracted by the pain that I was feeling. When I would get back to my hotel room, I would take off my shoes and socks and pray for my own healing. Immediately, the pain would diminish and within a few minutes would disappear completely. I would declare myself healed.

Since I am a spiritual person, I interpreted this event - in not just a natural way - but thought that it could be a work of the devil against me since it continued to reoccur. At a particular meeting - where I was on my feet for many hours - I was suffering from quite a lot of pain. I decided that I had had enough of this. I began to seek the Lord diligently about it in my hotel room after each meeting. Several times, I heard the word "socks." Since this did not make any sense to me, I dismissed it and continued to pray. However, each time the word "socks" came to me stronger. Finally, I asked the Lord about hearing the word "socks."

All of a sudden, I had a revelation- a realization- that my wife had, a few weeks before this, bought me new socks. I really liked them. They stayed up nicely because of elastic at the top of them. I realized, in that moment, that they were cutting off my circulation and that was causing my pain.

The Lord was telling me to get rid of the new socks and I would be healed. Amazing. Our God is not just the God of the supernatural but also of the natural. He is God of the Universe and the God of socks. Imagine this. God spoke to me about my socks.

Wheelchair-Bound Woman with MS Healed

I was preaching Christ as Healer at a large conference in Toronto, Canada. There were approximately 5,000 in attendance. After one of the services where many had received a healing, I was no longer engaged in praying for people after ministering healing for several hours. No one was coming any longer for prayer. I went to the back of the church stage to talk with one of the staff members of the church. As I was talking to him, two women beckoned me to come over to the edge of the stage so that they could speak with me. I responded by coming over to them. One of them said, "Would you pray with the woman in the wheelchair?" I said, "Of course." I came off the stage and went to the wheelchair.

This woman was not in the earlier service because she was in pain and distress, and decided to stay in her hotel room. When the other two women saw all the people being healed, they made her come to the service despite the fact that it was over from my perspective. This church has encouraged a practice of people laying on the carpet and praying for each other. This goes on long after services are done. Despite the service being over, there were still an estimated 500 people in the auditorium who were praying for each other.

I went over to the wheelchair and spent a few minutes being friendly and finding out about the situation that this woman was facing. She had full-blown MS. She had not walked and had been in the wheelchair for more than a decade. The only thing that she could feel in her legs was pain. One of her arms still worked but the other was held in a sling because it was dead-weight that would create pain in her shoulder. She could turn her head to the right but not to the left.

Shortly after interviewing her, I spent a few minutes telling her why I believed that Christ would heal her. I gave her a good dose of the Good News of Christ the Healer. I then laid hands on her and began to look to Jesus as her Healer. I asked her to make the confession, "This healing belongs to me because of what Jesus has done." Nothing was happening initially. I felt no healing happening.

If nothing is happening, this can be wrongly interpreted as meaning "God does not want to heal her." However, Christ healed all who came to Him in the multitudes. He never refused to heal anyone who came to Him in simple faith. If this woman had been in the multitudes, Christ would have healed her. Thankfully, the problem is never with Christ. The problem might be with me. It might be with the person who is trying to receive ministry. This is not to try to fix blame, as some might do. However, if you can't discover where the problem is, then you cannot fix it. I want to fix the problem so that healing happens. I am not interested in blaming anyone.

Since I was successfully helping people receive healing just a half hour before this, then I felt it was safe to assume that I was not the problem. This leaves the woman in the wheelchair. Prayerfully, I determined that she was having a hard time coming to Christ as Healer. I perceived that she was guilty over something. This is a common problem with Christians receiving healing. I asked her, "Are you connecting your MS with some event out of your past that makes you feel guilty?" She responded with "Yes." I told her that I did not need to know the details of that event but I suspected that she had confessed this as sin many times but still felt guilty over it. I reassured her that God forgave her the first time that she confessed this sin.

I then asked her to close her eyes and I told her that I was going to give her a parable of her forgiveness. I said, "You are standing before the throne of God with many thousands of God's people. Can you see this?" She said, "Yes." I said, "You are all wearing the righteous linen of the saints which is the righteousness of Christ. All of you are completely covered. All of you are completely forgiven. No one is more righteous than another. All have been completely received by God the Father because of what Christ has done. Can you see this?" She said, "Yes, I can see it."

Immediately after she said this, I had her say the healing confession again. "This healing belongs to me because of what Jesus has done." She said the confession and opened her eyes and, with enthusiasm, said, "My pain just left!" I said, "Wonderful. Would you like us to pray for the arm in the sling?" She said, "Yes!" I laid my hands lightly on her arm and within a few seconds, she confessed to the arm feeling very warm. Heat is a normal manifestation of healing. I got her two friends to take the arm out of the sling. Once the arm was out of the sling, I had her try it. Within seconds, she was moving the arm normally. At that point, the two women who had brought her to the service began to loudly praise God. This awoke the other 500 people in the auditorium to the fact that something was going on with the woman in the wheelchair. They began to gather around us.

Now when it was just the four of us (and Christ), healing was starting to happen with this woman. In general, it is easier to get people healed or delivered when just a few are praying. In the culture of the western church, faith for healing is still fragile and if you don't immediately get something happening in front of them, a crowd of Christians will slip back into doubt and unbelief. The doubt and unbelief of a crowd around you can make it harder to get people healed. (Jesus Christ could not do any miracles in Nazareth because of their unbelief. He was only able to heal a few sick people.)

When wheelchairs are involved, some are waiting for the dramatic moment to happen. They want you to jerk the person out of the wheelchair. (I have gotten many people healed who were in wheelchairs but they simply got healed while in the wheelchair and then just got out on their own because they were no longer sick and weak.)

I told the crowd watching that this woman had already received healing from God. She came in pain and was now pain free. She couldn't move the arm and now the arm was normal. I asked them to rejoice with me over this. I was preparing them to be patient with her to receive more partial healings. Partial healings most often lead to complete healings. In fact, when someone gets approximately half their healing, I believe that they often get to a "critical mass" of faith in Christ as Healer and get all the rest instantly.

I went back to speaking to the woman. I told her to ignore the people that were watching her. I then asked her if she would like to try to stand. She responded with "Yes." As her two friends moved the foot rests of the wheelchair to the sides and placed her feet on the ground, I laid my hands on her back. I asked her what she felt and she told me that she was feeling heat and electricity flow down her legs. I asked her to try to stand. She rocked back and forth in the wheelchair. As she did this, I asked her if she could have done that before. She said, "No." I made this report of her progress to the crowd to encourage them to continue to believe.

She then stood completely. I had my arm around her waist to steady her. She was still very weak and did not have her balance yet. The two women who had brought her to the service pushed the wheelchair back away from her. I asked her how long it had been since she had stood upright. It had been more than a decade. I asked her what she was feeling. She reported "heat and electricity" going down her legs.

I asked her if she was ready to take a step. She said, "Yes" and began to make an effort to move her left foot forward. She could not lift it so she tried to push it forward. After a minute or so, she had managed to get it a few inches in front of the other one. She then tried to pull the other foot forward. After another very long minute, she had succeeded in getting it in front of the other foot. I was still holding on to her waist because I did not want her to fall.

The second two steps came much more easily. The third two steps looked pretty normal and she seemed to have her balance. I let go of her and she began to walk very normally across the front of the auditorium. After about ten very normal steps, she then began to run around the edge of the auditorium with many of the people chasing her. She was completely free from MS. Jesus had completely healed her. From start to finish, 40 minutes had lapsed between the time that I came down from the stage to speak to her and when she began to run.

The 500 people who witnessed this healing then swamped me. It had triggered faith in Christ the Healer in them. For several hours, I witnessed the Lord healing many more people. Many received healing without prayer just through a momentary laying on of hands. It was the healing service after the healing service. Afterward, I went to my hotel room very tired but very aware and satisfied with the mercy and compassion of Christ the Healer. Two weeks later, I told this story in a healing meeting and there was another wheelchair-bound woman with MS who received a complete healing in a very similar fashion. Thank you, Lord Jesus.

Getting Mom Healed

Back a few years ago, my friends and colleagues in ministry, Tom and Jody. were having lunch with my wife Ann and me. Tom and Jody started sharing some of their frustration at getting Tom's mother healed. Tom's elderly mother was not a strong believer but didn't resist the idea of being healed. While I don't remember the exact words, it was something like, "Roger, we don't understand why we can go out with you to a healing meeting and just about everyone we pray for receives healing, but we can't seem to get Mom healed despite praying for her many times."

I said to them, "Well, what are you doing different than what we do when we do a healing meeting?" They thought about it and one of them said, "I don't think that we are doing anything different." I said, "That may be true, but consider we don't pray for people for healing unless they have heard me preach the Good News about Christ the Healer for at least an hour. Have you shared the Good News about Jesus the Healer with your mom?" They said to me, 'I guess we haven't really done that." So I said, "Well, try that and see if it produces a different result." Within a few days of that event, they had, first of all, shared the Good News about Jesus the Healer with Mom and then had prayed for her. She received a complete healing on that occasion.

Tom's mother felt so good afterward, she decided to go on a vacation to visit some friends and relatives in California. While she was there, one of her friends shared that they were in deep pain caused by some ailment. She said to them, "Let me share with you what Tom told me about Jesus," and shared briefly about Jesus the Healer with her relative in pain. Mom then laid her hands on her friend and they were healed. Now mom had very little Bible knowledge but did understand that Christ had died for her sickness. Sharing the Good News with her friend enabled her faith to rise to the occasion and for her to minister healing to her friend.

If prayer is not working for you, try soaking in the Good News about Christ the Healer. If you don't have a harvest yet, plant more seed.

Korean Wife Hears Christ Speak

During the time that I was an Artillery Officer - before I became an Army Chaplain - I had the opportunity on a field training exercise to share the Good News with my new driver. He prayed and received Christ as Savior in our vehicle. He was born again. Within a few weeks of that time, he was baptized in water and received the Baptism in the Holy Spirit. He was now able to pray in a supernatural prayer language, which is often called "speaking in tongues."

He had recently returned from being stationed in South Korea. During that time, he had married a Korean woman. She seemed very nice. However, she did not speak English and my driver didn't speak Korean very well. She was also a practicing Buddhist. He had tried to explain to her what had happened to him. She didn't understand what had happened to her husband, but she was not opposing it.

There was a "Charismatic" style worship service that happened every Sunday night. Often during that service, people came to the altar to pray. One evening, my driver and his wife were in attendance. He went to the altar to pray and she followed along - just to be with him - and knelt at the altar with him.

There were quite a few who had come to the altar to pray. My driver was to the left of his wife and there was another man on her right. Because she had come along to the altar, my driver was inspired to pray for her salvation.

After a few minutes, the man on her right started speaking in fluent Korean to her. However, he never looked at her. He simply looked like he was praying. He called her by name. He told her that she was loved by God. He told her that Christ had died for her sins. He told her that she could receive forgiveness of her sins. He told her that she could have a brand new life with God by believing in Jesus. There was more. Several times, he used her name.

Finally, curiosity overwhelmed her. She tapped him on the shoulder. He turned towards her. She asked him in Korean how he knew her. He looked puzzled and then recognized that she was Korean. He said, "I am sorry but I don't speak Korean." He had been speaking in his supernatural prayer language to God. He didn't know Korean but the Holy Spirit did and used him to speak to her. When she discovered that God had been speaking to her in this amazing way, she received Christ as her Savior.

Two Women in Wheelchairs Healed

In Colorado, I was preaching Christ as Healer in a meeting. There were two women in wheelchairs sitting on the left and right sides of the front row of chairs. I usually allow the Good News about Christ as Healer to do its divine work of creating and releasing faith in Christ as Healer to bring people forward. If people are able, it is better for them to respond in faith to Christ and come forward than for me to seek them out for prayer. The vast majority of the people in multitudes who received healing came to Christ in simple faith that He would help them. This is why the Gospels record Christ saying "Your faith has healed you" or something very similar 18 times.

One of these women in wheelchairs indicated - by coming forward - that she wanted ministry. I interviewed her briefly and she told me that she had been wheelchair-bound for a number of years because she had severe rheumatoid arthritis. She went on to say that her joints were all damaged by this disease - painful, stiff, and swollen - and were getting worse.

I laid hands on her shoulders and had her make the confession, "This healing belongs to me because of what Jesus has done." She did this and I felt heat on her shoulders. I asked her if she felt it and she indicated that she was feeling heat all over her body. In a few minutes, she decided - on her own - that she wanted to get out of the wheelchair. She slowly accomplished this and began to walk around.

I asked her how she was doing. Her answer was "much better." I let her continue to walk around and I went back to praying for people. In about 15 minutes, I observed that she was walking around very normally - much better than before - and she seemed to be checking all her joints by moving those parts of her body. I asked her again how she was doing. She said, "All the stiffness and pain is gone. The swelling in my hands is gone." She showed me her hands. I had not paid attention to what they had looked like before so I didn't know how much they had changed. However, I did believe her. I said, "I think that you are healed. What do you think?" She smiled and said, "Oh yes. Jesus has healed me."

This healing seemed to motivate the other woman in the wheelchair. She came forward for ministry. I interviewed her and she said that she also had severe rheumatoid arthritis. I laid my hands on her and intended for her to do the confession, "This healing belongs to me because of what Jesus has done" but before I could ask her to do this, I felt an evil spirit go out of her. She said with great excitement, "I felt it leave!" and immediately got out of the wheelchair. She was walking normally, bending, and raising her arms to check out her healing.

I am sure that the people watching thought that they had seen a miracle but it was actually a deliverance from an evil spirit. This evil spirit had mimicked rheumatoid arthritis. I am not even sure that the woman knew that it was an evil spirit causing her sickness but I became aware of it as it left her. She said, "I felt it leave!" She might have meant "I felt the sickness leave" rather than "I felt an evil spirit leave."

Sometimes this story creates questions in people. For instance, do you have to know beforehand if an evil spirit is creating the sickness? The answer is no if you minister the way that I do. I preach Jesus Christ as Healer. I invite people to come to Christ for healing. When they come in simple faith, they will meet Jesus in the way that they need to meet Him. He knows if they simply need physical healing or if they need deliverance from an evil spirit. They get what they need from Him. So, generally speaking, I do not need to know in advance what is causing the sickness. Jesus knows and that is enough. He is both our Healer and our Deliverer. Thank you, Lord Jesus.

Healing of the Acadian

My 83-year-old father was hospitalized in Houston due to weakness. This was his only symptom. There was quite a bit of speculation as to why this was happening, and much medical testing that did not reveal a particular problem. After a few days without any diagnosis of a problem, I came down to assist my family in being with him at the hospital. At first, he was not exceptionally weak and would get up and walk around the medical floor for some exercise. On one of these walks, I was walking with him.

After walking a bit, he sat down where there was a group of chairs. There was a man sitting there whom my father had met before I had arrived at the hospital. He was in a room next to my father's room on the right side. My father and this man had something in common. They had both been in the petroleum business. This particular man was from Southern Louisiana and was of French descent. People of this ethnic group are generally Roman Catholic by birth. They refer to themselves as "Acadian" or the shortened version "Cajun."

My father introduced me to the man and eventually said to him, "My son gets people healed when he prays for them. Would you like him to pray for you?"

The man, without hesitation, said, "Yes, I would like him to pray for me." I asked him about his condition and he told me that he had come to the hospital for some sort of chest surgery. The surgery had gone well but he had developed a serious infection in the surgical wound. He described it as "seven hot spots" of infection. They had, for several weeks, used an arsenal of various medications on the infection but it had gotten much worse. He had been told that there was nothing else for them to do. They had told him that he didn't have long to live. They were arranging for him to transfer to hospice care.

After he told me this, I spent a few minutes sharing the Good News with him. He seemed very absorbed in what I was saying. When I was done, I laid my hands very lightly on his chest and got him to repeat the confession, "This healing belongs to me because of what Jesus has done." He repeated this and I felt a moderate flow of heat to his chest. I told him that I thought that he had received healing. He nodded in agreement.

The next morning, this man excitedly came into my father's room. He told us that when they had inspected the infection just a few minutes before, they had told him that all the infection seemed to be gone except for one small area. He said that he knew during the night that something was very different because he felt the wound drain. The small area of infection disappeared that day. Jesus Christ had healed him. This man was very excited and went up and down the hallway on this medical floor declaring that he had met a healer. He was speaking about me. When I heard this, I gently corrected him and said, "Yes. His name is Jesus." He did stir up a man with a sick wife to ask me for prayer and she was also healed.

Later that day, this Acadian man asked if he could speak to me privately. I agreed and we went to his room. He bowed his head and said to me, "Father, bless me for I have sinned." He was reacting to me as if I was a Roman

Catholic priest and he was asking for forgiveness. I asked him to pray with me and he confessed his sins and received Christ as His Savior. Within a day or so of this event, he was released from the hospital to go home.

My father went on to be with the Lord shortly thereafter. He was not sick, but got weaker, simply went to sleep, and woke up in the presence of the Lord.

Healing of Alzheimer's Disease

As a result of my 83-year-old father being hospitalized in Houston for weakness, I was involved in the healing of a man with a life-threatening infection in a surgical wound. When this man was healed, he became very vocal about it and announced on the hospital floor that he had been healed. This stirred up an elderly man in the room on the left side of my father's room to seek me out to minister to his elderly wife. I don't remember exactly what she was hospitalized for, but she also had full-blown Alzheimer's Disease.

I told this elderly man that I would be glad to pray for his wife but would be delayed for several hours because I was going to be with my father as he went for more diagnostic tests. In the meantime, I convinced the elderly man to watch some of my healing DVDs on a portable DVD player that my father and I were using in his room. The reason that I did this is because the Good News about Christ the Healer has the ability to release the right kind of faith in Christ for people to receive healing.

After the tests were over and my father was back in his room, I went to the room where this man and his wife were located. I asked the man if he had understood the DVDs, and he told me that he and his wife were life-long Christians, and he believed that the Lord would heal his wife. He and I laid our hands on her and he repeated the confession, "This healing belongs to her because of what Jesus has done." I don't remember feeling anything in particular.

The next day, this man happily declared to me that his wife was much better. The day after that, he told me that his wife was no longer sick. The third day, he came in to my father's room, wept, and said, "The Lord has given my wife back to me. She no longer has Alzheimer's." Jesus had healed her.

As a result of the two healings, my father asked me, "Do you think that I am in the hospital so that you could pray for these people?" I said, "Dad, I think that the reason that you are in the hospital is because you are feeling weak, but God can use anything." My father went on to be with the Lord a few weeks later. He was not sick. He just got weaker and went to sleep and woke up in the presence of the Lord.

Injured Surfer Receives Healing

The senior leader of a church in another English-speaking country asked me to minister in a "Youth Church" on a Sunday evening. He recommended that I keep my message short and do a demonstration that God would heal the sick and injured fairly quickly, or I might lose the attention of the young people.

There were about 300 young people in attendance. From the stage, I preached the shortest Good News message that I had ever done in front of a group of people. I estimate that I spoke for 10 minutes. I explained what Christ had accomplished on the cross concerning healing. I explained how He had demonstrated the will of the Father in healing by healing all who came to Him in simple faith. I seemed to have the attention of these young people.

I then moved to doing a demonstration that God would heal the injured. I asked for a volunteer who had some sort of painful injury - a bad back, a bad shoulder, an arm that could not be raised, or bad knees - that was ready to be healed. No one responded. Since my American-Texan English would have seemed highly accented to these young people, I asked again but slower and spoke each word more carefully. Again, there was no response. At this point, I silently asked the Lord for help in getting a volunteer. As I did this, a young man who appeared to me to be about 16 years old came forward out of the crowd and came up the stairs slowly to the stage where I was standing. His body language told me that he was showing off for the other young people.

He came to me on the stage. I interviewed him briefly as the other young people listened. He did have a recent injury to his back due to some sort of surfing mishap. He could not bend very far without feeling a lot of pain. He demonstrated this by bending only slightly at the waist and grimacing in pain.

I laid my hands on his back and had him repeat the confession, "This healing belongs to me because of what Jesus has done." He made the confession and I felt quite a bit of heat go into his back for the next 5 seconds or so. I asked him if he felt the heat and he said that he did feel it. I said to him, "Try bending again." This time, without effort, he bent completely and touched his feet with his hands and came back up with a surprised look on his face and said the "s-word" very loudly.

I started laughing, the senior leader was laughing, and all the young people were laughing. He was standing there with a look of surprise and wonder on his face. I said to him, "Do it again." He bent down again and put his palms flat on the floor and stayed there for a second or two. He then came up and said the "s-word" very loudly again.

Everyone was still laughing in reaction to his surprise and him expressing it in this way. However, the surprise on his face changed to stark terror. I tried to get him to come towards me but he was back-pedaling away from me. I wanted him to tell us that there was no pain any longer. I wanted him to give us details of how bad the back was before we prayed in comparison. However, he wasn't going to come close to me. He jumped off the stage and ran out of the building with dozens of young people in pursuit. They eventually ran him down and got him to receive Christ as Savior.

The next day, the senior leader and I were having lunch together. He said, "We got calls from all over the country about that healing." Puzzled, I said, "How did people know about it?" He said, "You weren't aware that we were broadcasting that meeting on live television?" I laughed and said, "No." He went on to say that because this young man had used the "s-word" twice in conjunction to his healing, people who saw the healing knew that it was not being faked. Thank you, Jesus.

Creative Miracle Restores Missing Ear Organs

A few months back, I took a healing team to a nearby state. On Friday evening, after I preached Jesus Christ as Healer, we ministered to a man who was born without the normal physical organs for hearing in one of his ears. Because he did have the auditory nerves in that ear, as a small child, they surgically implanted two small bones against the nerve. This provided him with 10% hearing and a lifetime of pain in that ear. On that night, just after prayer for him, he received an increase in hearing and the pain disappeared. He testified to having an estimated 50% hearing in that ear.

The next morning, he was doing his morning hygiene. As he cleaned that ear, the two small bones that had been implanted in his ear fell out. He felt a major change in his ear and discovered that his hearing had been restored completely. He received 100% hearing in that ear complete with the missing organs and no pain. He gave us this report on Sunday morning. Thank you, Jesus.

Roger Sapp Receives Healing of Cancer

One of my sons was diagnosed with colon cancer in April 2009. He is now cancer-free and is doing well. As a result of my son's diagnosis of colon cancer, I made an appointment to do a colonoscopy. I was overdue, since at my age, they are recommended every five years. When an initial blood test was run, my PSA (Prostate Specific Antigen) was 3.4. While this is still in the normal range, it was quite a rapid rise over my PSA of 2.1 in November of 2008. Apparently, a rapid rise in PSA is a signal that things are not good with the prostate gland. In late April, I had a colonoscopy coupled with a biopsy of my prostate gland. They found no problems with my colon. They took 36 biopsy samples of my prostate gland. A small percentage of a single sample showed cancer with a Gleason scale of 7 (3,4.) I had no symptoms of a prostate problem. A follow-up bone scan found that there had been no spread of the cancer to other organs which is an ongoing threat of prostate cancer. I was diagnosed with stage 1 prostate cancer. I thoroughly educated myself on what medical treatments were available and what the outcome of these treatments might be. Most of the medical treatments available call for the complete destruction of the prostate gland either by surgery, radiation or by freezing the tissue. These medical treatments are life-changing for a man and the cancer may return. The life expectancy of a man who does these treatments and a man who does nothing are nearly the same.

I broke into full-time healing ministry in the early 90's largely because of daily meditation on Christ as Healer for two years. Since that time, I have seen the Lord heal more than 30,000 people. In April 2009, I decided to meditate on Christ for my own healing. I had created a deck of healing meditation cards for that purpose. I used these cards to meditate on Christ, seek Him, and confess my faith in Christ in my private times with the Lord. Typically this was for an hour each morning but sometimes, I carried the deck around with me and if I was waiting for something or standing in a line, I pulled out the cards and began to meditate. I kept some cards in my car. If I was stuck in traffic, I began to meditate. I had some cards in the bathroom. You get the picture.

I had my friends Tom and Jody Chauvin pray for me privately. I also received public prayer at a meeting in Colorado in team ministry with friends Brian and Mary Crews. On both occasions of praying with others, I felt a tingle of power in the appropriate region of my body. On July 29, the results of another PSA test came back at 1.7 which is lower than the 2.1 that I had in November 2008. It is half of what I had in April 2009. At that time, I felt that this was an encouragement to continue to pray and to postpone any medical treatment. On Sept 28, a PSA test came back at 1.3 which is unheard of with someone who has been diagnosed with prostate cancer. It is also very low for a man my age without cancer. I have had several more very low PSA tests all under 1.7 in January and March. Since that time, I have had many more PSA tests and they have all come back with a very low numbers. As of the writing of this book in July 2013, four years after my diagnosis with cancer, I have no symptoms. I have done nothing medical. I work out regularly. I am strong, healthy and productive for Christ the King. Thank you, Jesus, for being my Healer.

Biography of Roger Sapp

Roger Sapp received Christ as his Savior and Baptizer in the Holy Spirit in a Youth With A Mission coffeehouse ministry for American soldiers in former West Germany in 1972. For the next twenty years, his experience of physical healing was unpredictable, unreliable, and mysterious. In 1993, he had a breakthrough that changed his understanding of healing by focusing him on Christ as the perfect example of healing ministry. Since that time, more than thirty-thousand healings, deliverances, and creative miracles have accompanied his ministry

.
For the past fifteen years, he has been equipping other believers to do Christ-like healing. He is the author of ten books and many booklets and articles. His most popular books are **Performing Miracles and Healing**, a comprehensive biblical guide to developing a Christ-like supernatural ministry, **Beyond a Shadow of a Doubt**, a shorter book dealing with the doubts that block healing and **Paid in Full,** a radical series of three books on grace in biblical finances.

His background includes the Eagle Scout award earned in his youth. He has served local churches as an elder, assistant pastor and pastor. He has been an Army Artillery officer, a prison, hospital, troop and pastor chaplain. He honorably retired from the U.S. Army in 1993 and was a theology professor until 1997. He holds earned Bachelor, Master of Divinity and Doctor of Philosophy degrees.

Many have commented favorably on Dr. Sapp's relaxed style of ministry. He was frequently a guest speaker at the Toronto Airport Christian Fellowship. He has appeared as a guest on their television program. He has been a guest on several national Christian radio programs including Sid Roth's Messianic Vision and his television program "It's Supernatural." He has spoken in more than 300 churches worldwide during the last two decades.

Dr. Sapp presently travels full-time in ministry by invitation of local churches, conferences and house churches. He is associated with and recommended by the leaders of several networks of churches. He is the founder of the Guardian House Church Network. He has been happily married to his high-school sweetheart, Ann, since 1970. They and their grown children and their spouses live in the Dallas/Fort Worth area. Dr. Sapp can be reached at 1-817-514-0653, All Nations Ministries, P.O. Box 620, Springtown, Texas 76082 USA, website: **www.allnationsmin.org** or by email at **contact@allnationsmin.org**.

36771018R00076

Made in the USA
Charleston, SC
17 December 2014